Soso Parebul
(ɛn ɔda oku tɔk)

na Dafni Balat Prat gɛda dɛn

KRIO PROVERBS AND IDIOMS
Collected By
Daphne Barlatt Pratt

Edited by

Blanche Gooding

Sierra Leonean Writers Series

Soso Parebul

(Ɛn Ɔda Oku Tɔk)

ISBN: 978-99910-54-70-4

Cover designed by: Harold Creighton-Randall

Sierra Leonean Writers Series

DIS BUK YA NA FƆ

Ɔl mi Salon Brɔda Ɛn Sista dɛn

TƐNKI

a tɛl tɛnki to mi man, Tanimɔla Prat, mi pikin dɛn we na Harold ɛn Olayinka Creighton-Randall, ɛn mi granpikin dɛn we na Quanuah, Eula ɛn Enam Creighton-Randall.

a tɛl tɛnki to ɔl dɛn pipul ya we rid di parebul dɛn, ɛn tɛl mi if a mis pan aw a rayt dɛn, ɔ pan wetin a tink se dɛn min.

Rev. Elijah Akibo-Jones
Mrs. Ellen Cline-Cole
Mr. Dan Cole
Mrs. Olayinka Creighton-Randall
Professor Eldred Jones
Mr. Frank Karefa-Smart
Miss Margidu Turner
Mrs Blanche Gooding

a tɛl dɛn bɔku bɔku tɛnki fɔ we dɛn peshɛnt wit mi, dɛn nɔ taya fɔ ɛp mi te ɔltin dɔn. a pre mek Gɔd blɛs dɛn ɔl.

dɛn a wan tɛl tɛnki to mi pɔblisha Mallam O, fɔ ɔl di bɔku imel ɛn tɛks mɛsej we go ɔp ɛn dɔŋ ɔp ɛn dɔŋ bitwin wi tu, we insɛf bin de ɛp mi. nɔto kɔmɔn ɛp i ɛp mi.

Guide to Pronunciation

Krio consonant sounds – same as in English

Krio vowels – **a e i o u ɛ ɔ**

Every Krio letter has its own sound which does not change.

One letter – one sound. Always the same sound.

Vowels	Krio	English
a – as in at	at	at
e – as in eight; ate	et	eight; ate
i – as in it (I = i)	it	it
o – as in oh	bot	boat
u – as in put	put	put
ɛ – as in eh	gɛt/gɛ	get
ɔ – as in or	kɔn	corn

<u>Also</u>

	Krio	English
aw	kaw	cow
ay	day	die
ɔy	bɔy	boy

<u>In Krio,</u>		Krio	English
	c=k	kaw	cow
	X=ks	aks	axe
	ŋ	Fritɔŋ	Freetown
		tɔŋ	tongue
		kiŋ	king

iv

KRIO PROVERBS

Proverbs talk about what a group of people living together as a nation or tribe, think about life. Krio proverbs talk about what the people see happening around them, and about behavioural patterns. Some try to give rules to govern human behaviour, and others state the repercussions of deviating from the behavioural norms of the group. In days gone by, our proverbs were much used by our ancestors in everyday life, to teach children, and help kinsmen, to conform to the norms of the group. That, however, is dying out, and the present generation, especially the many who have emigrated, are forgetting this part of our culture and language.

I have been collecting Krio proverbs for well over thirty years, and have now written them down so that our children and future generations will not lose this rich part of our heritage. In this collection, I have used proverbs from:

1. *The Picture of Krio Life.* Freetown 1900 – 1920 by H. Kreutzinger, edited by Engelbert Stiglmayr. Wien – (1968)
2. *A Krio – English Dictionary*, compiled by Clifford N. Fyle and Eldred D. Jones.

Published by Oxford University Press (1980)

3. *Fishing in Rivers of Sierra Leone*, edited by H. Hinzen, F.B. James, J.M. Sorie, S.A.T. Tamu. Published by People's Educational Association of Sierra leone. (1987)

4. *Parables From Kossoh Town by King Creole.* Pub by Kings Promotions. (1991)

5. *Lɛ Wi Lan Krio - JSS1* by Nathaniel Pearce and Ruby Pearce. Edited by CN Fyle. Published by Lekon Publishing (1996)

6. *Fambul dɛm, una kushɛ, o. An Introduction to Sierra Leone Krio and its Writing Systems.* Emile C.M.K. Jones. GLOM (201ɛ)

and other oral sources got from a host of elderly members in the community.

Each proverb, known as parable 'parebul' in Krio, is written in Krio, followed by a translation into English, and then the interpretation, or probable application is given in English. Sometimes there are several interpretations, depending on the situation in which the proverb is being applied. And of course proverbs being enigmatic use of language, the link between the proverb and its application might sometimes seem obscure. The translation is, as far as is possible, a WORD FOR

WORD translation, which is most definitely not a good way of translating. I have however decided to do it this way, to help the many who are fluent in English, but do not know Krio very well. It is designed to help them to know the exact meaning in English, of a particular Krio word. Hence the 'word for word' translation i.e each English word more or less, as far as is possible, corresponding to its Krio counterpart. In some cases, the word for word translation gives an interpretation which is misleading. Then the translation has to be more flexible.

This word for word translation is often not the most fluent Engish, but in most cases, it gives a clear idea of what is said, while identifying each Krio word with its English counterpart in meaning. e.g.

da lif we swit na got mɔt na in de rɔn in bɛlɛ.

That leaf which is sweet in goat's mouth it is it which runs its belly.

A better translation would be:

The leaf which the goat finds most delicious, is the

one which gives it diarrhoea.

I have deliberately not translated this way, as I've explained, to help non fluent Krio speakers to have a better understanding of the language, and how we arrive at what we say.

Included here, are some proverbs which are very much part of the language, but are not used in polite company. I am however convinced that they should not be excluded from this collection, because they are historically, and a bona-fide part of the Sierra Leone Krio Language.

PAREBUL

parebul de tɔk bɔt wetin pɔsin dɛn we tap togɛda na wan neshɔn ɔ na wan trayb, tink bɔt layf. dɛn de tɔk bɔt wetin dɛn si se de apin na layf, ɛn aw mɔtalman tan. dɛn de tray fɔ tɛl dɛn kɔmpin mɔtalman aw fɔ biev, ɛn de wɔn wetin go apin if pɔsin biev wan kayn we, ɔ du sɔnkayn tin. wi lɔntɛm pipul dɛn kin de tek parebul tren pikin. dat nɔ so de naw, ɛn wi pipul dɛn de fɔgɛt wi parebul dɛn. a de kan rayt sɔm dɔŋ, sodat wi pikin dɛn go sabi dɛn, ɛn dɛn ɔl nɔ go day go wit wi.

Each parable is written in three parts, as follows:

1. Krio parebul
2. Literal word-for-word translation into English – L
3. Interpretation
4. Reader's Exercise (If you have a different interpretation that you would like the author to consider in a future edition of this book, please send an email to: sosoparebul-feedback@gmail.com)

ix

Krio Proverbs and Idioms (Daphne Barlatt Pratt)

1. Krio Parebul	a dɔn pul bɔd na trap we in yay rɛd lɛk jembetutu, so nɔto pɛpɛ bɔd de kan mek chwi chwi chwi pan mi.
Literal Translation	I have removed a bird with eyes as red as jembetutu (kind of brown dove) from a trap. So 'pepper bird' cannot come and make, 'twi twi twi' at me.
Interpretation	I am not frightened by, and can easily cope with a small matter like this, for I have coped with much more dangerous situations.
Exercise: Reader's Interpretation	
2. Krio Parebul	a nɔ go day fɔ pɛpɛ we sɔl de.
Literal Translation	I will not die for pepper when salt is there
Interpretation	One need not distress oneself because of the unavailability of inessentials when the necessary and essential things are available.
Exercise: Reader's Interpretation	
3. Krio Parebul	a nɔ go dɔn de wit yu na wekin ol nɛt dɛn na mɔnin yu aks wetin mek mi yay rɛd.
Literal Translation	I would not have been with you at a wake all night, and then in the morning you ask why my eyes are red.

1

Interpretation	We were both in the situation which has caused me to look, feel or act the way I do, so why ask for explanations.
Exercise: Reader's Interpretation	
4. Krio Parebul	**a nɔ go dɔn sɛl naynti-nayn grani a nɔ no mi yon grani in prays.**
Literal Translation	I cannot have sold ninety-nine grandmothers and I do not know my own grandmother's price.
Interpretation	Of course I know everything about the subject in question because I have had a lot of experience in such matters.
Exercise: Reader's Interpretation	
5. Krio Parebul	**a nɔ go fala pikin drɔ kalbas.**
Literal Translation	I will not follow a child to pull a calabash. (play tug-of-war with a calabash)
Interpretation	I refuse to demean myself by quarrelling with a child especially when such a quarrel might have unpleasant or disastrous results. (calabash being easily smashed.)
Exercise: Reader's Interpretation	

6. Krio Parebul	a nɔ go gɛ lif a tek mi an tot shit. (a nɔ go lɛf lif na bush a tek mi an wep mi wes.)
Literal Translation	I will not have a leaf and take my hand to hold faeces.
Interpretation	I will not have the wherewithal at hand to do something and not use it, but continue to suffer.
Exercise: Reader's Interpretation	
7. Krio Parebul	a nɔ it bif so a nɔ go kaka ia. (na udat it bif de shit ia.)
Literal Translation	I have not eaten meat so I will not excrete hair.
Interpretation	I have not committed the act which results in such consequences so I will not suffer those consequences.
Exercise: Reader's Interpretation	
8. Krio Parebul	adu tɛnki nɔ bay plaba.
Literal Translation	How do, thank you, does not buy palaver.
Interpretation	The exchange of greetings smoothens relationships.
Exercise: Reader's Interpretation	
9. Krio Parebul	aks fɔ ed yu se a go Grama Skul.

Literal Translation	Ask for head, you say you went to The Grammar School.
Interpretation	Instead of asking for good luck, you rely on your privileged background to succeed in life.
Exercise: Reader's Interpretation	
10. Krio Parebul	**an go an kam.**
Literal Translation	Hand go hand come.
Interpretation	Help is given and received.
Exercise: Reader's Interpretation	
11. Krio Parebul	**arata na big mɔreman bɔt i nɔ go pre na pus kanda.**
Literal Translation	The rat is a big (important) muslim soothsayer, but it will not pray on a cat's skin.
Interpretation	A person always knows, or should know, how far he can dare.
Exercise: Reader's Interpretation	
12. Krio Parebul	**arata nɔ de day i nɔ shek tel.**
Literal Translation	A rat does not die without shaking its tail.
Interpretation	making one last desperate effort before giving up a fight.

Exercise: Reader's Interpretation	
13. Krio Parebul	**arata nɔ go kɔt nyanga usay pus de.**
Literal Translation	A rat will not go showing off, where there is a cat.
Interpretation	You will not go showing off where there are people who have the power to harm you.
Exercise: Reader's Interpretation	
14. Krio Parebul	**as fɔ trɔbul bɛtɛ pas as fɔ bɛrin.**
Literal Translation	Hush for trouble is better than hush for bereavement. Hush– expressing sympathy.
Interpretation	It is preferable to express sympathy for misfortune rather than for bereavement.
Exercise: Reader's Interpretation	
15. Krio Parebul	**at noto bon.**
Literal Translation	Heart is not bone.
Interpretation	There is a limit to what the heart can take.

Exercise: Reader's Interpretation	
16. Krio Parebul	**aw di bata de bit na so di egugu de dans.**
Literal Translation	How the bata is beating, that's how the egugu is dancing.(bata– small drum. egugu–masked devil)
Interpretation	To every action there is an appropriate response. Circumstances determine one's actions.
Exercise: Reader's Interpretation	
17. Krio Parebul	**aw fa kɔtintri to lɛmon gras.**
Literal Translation	How far is the cotton tree from lemon grass.
Interpretation	There is a very wide social gap/ difference in academc achievement/or material possessions between those two individuals or groups of people.
Exercise: Reader's Interpretation	
18. Krio Parebul	**aw yu mek yu bed na so yu go ledɔm de.**
Literal Translation	How you make your bed that's how you will lie down in it.
Interpretation	You will suffer the consequences of your actions.

Exercise: Reader's Interpretation	
19. Krio Parebul	**awuf nɔ gɛ bɔn.**
Literal Translation	Something which is free does not have any bone. (no bones in it)
Interpretation	Things obtained free are pleasant to enjoy. One tends to overindulge when something is free.
Exercise: Reader's Interpretation	
20. Krio Parebul	**ayɛn na in de kɔt ayɛn.**
Literal Translation	Iron is what cuts iron.
Interpretation	A tough adversary can only be defeated by someone of equal strength. One's worthy efforts are equal to the measure of the difficulty.
Exercise: Reader's Interpretation	
21. Krio Parebul	**babu lɛk ala you go gi am wachman wok.**
Literal Translation	The baboon likes to shout, you go and give him watchman's work
Interpretation	Putting someone in a situation in which he can indulge in a particular habit.
Exercise: Reader's Interpretation	
22. Krio Parebul	**babu lɛk klin grɔn.**

Literal Translation	The baboon likes clean ground.
Interpretation	Those who are undeserving like to have good things they haven't worked for. Someone aspiring to acquire something of quality for which he hasn't worked.
Exercise: Reader's Interpretation	
23. Krio Parebul	**babu na babu lɛpɛt na lɛpɛt.**
Literal Translation	A baboon is a baboon, a leopard is a leopard.
Interpretation	Different people (or animals) have different characteristics which do not change, so one should accept the fact of what they are, and not expect anything different. / We all have our different distinct identifiable characteristics, either at social, tribal or national level, so one should accept that fact.
Exercise: Reader's Interpretation	
24. Krio Parebul	**bad bush nɔ de fɔ trowe bad pikin.**
Literal Translation	There is no bad bush to throw away a bad child.

Interpretation	No matter what a child does, its own parents cannot wash their hands off it. Hence, in close relationships, one should strive to forgive and preserve the bond. Don't 'throw away' the offender.
Exercise: Reader's Interpretation	
25. Krio Parebul	**bad man bɛtɛ pas ɛmti os. (luk – push yanda bɛtɛ pas ɛmti bed)**
Literal Translation	A bad man is better than an empty house.
Interpretation	It is better to have a husband, no matter how bad he is, than be alone/ lonely/ be without 'protection'/security, with no male around. He must be useful at doing something.
Exercise: Reader's Interpretation	
26. Krio Parebul	**bad mɛrɛsin na in fɔ tek mɛn bad sofut. (luk– tranga sik want tranga mɛrɛsin.)**
Literal Translation	bad medicine is what should be taken to mend (heal) a bad sore on the foot.
Interpretation	Tough measures are needed to tackle difficult situations.

Exercise: Reader's Interpretation	
27. Krio Parebul	**banana dɔn gɛ wata bifo ren kam.**
Literal Translation	The banana already had water before rain came. (before it rained)
Interpretation	Someone was born privileged, so is not impressed with newly acquired wealth or status. Also, not easily affected by the vicissitudes of life because one's position has been long established.
Exercise: Reader's Interpretation	
28. Krio Parebul	**bay ɛn sɛl nɔto plaba.**
Literal Translation	Buying and selling is not palaver.
Interpretation	trader and customer should conduct their business in an amicable manner. Doing business should not be a cause for disagreement.
Exercise: Reader's Interpretation	
29. Krio Parebul	**beg sɔl nɔ de kuk sup.**
Literal Translation	Begged salt does not cook soup.

Interpretation	You cannot depend on begging to amass enough to do what you want to do. What a gift can accomplish is limited, so exert self effort to get enough of what you need.
Exercise: Reader's Interpretation	
30. Krio Parebul	**bɛlɛ nɔ gɛt lukinglas.**
Literal Translation	The belly does not have a looking glass. (mirror).
Interpretation	You have to take responsibility for what you eat and not expect your system to warn you what is bad for you.
Exercise: Reader's Interpretation	
31. Krio Parebul	**bɛlɛ nɔ gɛ tɛnki.**
Literal Translation	The stomach does not have thank you.
Interpretation	The stomach is never satisfied. It will always want more sooner or later.
Exercise: Reader's Interpretation	
32. Krio Parebul	**biabia man nɔ de fityay drɔsup.**
Literal Translation	A man who has a beard does not disrespect drawsoup.(drɔsup – okra or krenkre–leaves cooked with palmoil and different kinds of meat into a thick sticky soup.)

11

Interpretation	Depending on your circumstances, always act with caution in certain situations.
Exercise: Reader's Interpretation	
33. Krio Parebul	**biabia man nɔ de mek padi wit faya.**
Literal Translation	A man with a beard does not make friends with fire.
Interpretation	Be aware of what you are and be careful not to put yourself in situations which may be dangerous to you.
Exercise: Reader's Interpretation	
34. Krio Parebul	**bifo banana lif disgres, na raysbred go gɛt ɔmbak.**
Literal Translation	(Before) Rather than the banana leaf being disgraced, it is ricebread which will have a hunched back.
Interpretation	One is prepared to do whatever it takes to prevent failure. Go to any length to ensure that what is being done turns out successfully.
Exercise: Reader's Interpretation	
35. Krio Parebul	**bifo bɔd flay yu no ɔmɔs eg de na in bɛlɛ.**

Literal Translation	Before a bird flies you know how many eggs are in its belly.
Interpretation	As soon as you hear the merest hint or whisper of something you presume to know all the facts about it.
Exercise: Reader's Interpretation	
36. Krio Parebul	**bifo fut na in biɛn fut de fala.**
Literal Translation	The before foot is the one that the behind foot follows.
Interpretation	We follow the example of our elders and betters. e.g. older siblings, parents, teachers and others in authority.
Exercise: Reader's Interpretation	
37. Krio Parebul	**bifo gud it wes na bɛlɛ go bɔs.**
Literal Translation	Before good food is wasted, it is the belly which will burst.
Interpretation	A good natural way of welcoming an abundance of food. / Overeating with the excuse that you don't want to waste good food.
Exercise: Reader's Interpretation	
38. Krio Parebul	**bifo i bɔn lɛ i wɛt.**
Literal Translation	Before it burns let it get wet.

Interpretation	The lesser of two evils. Better to cause a minor disaster inorder to avoid a major one.
Exercise: Reader's Interpretation	

39. Krio Parebul	**bifo krawo wes na spun go bɛn.**
Literal Translation	Before krawo wastes, it is the spoon which will be bent. (krawo–crust left at the bottom of pot of food)
Interpretation	Getting something done even if there are adverse effects. The cost of achieving a goal.
Exercise: Reader's Interpretation	

40. Krio Parebul	**bifo ɔs na in biɛn wan de fala.**
Literal Translation	Before horse (the one that is in front) is the one behind one is following.
Interpretation	The younger follow the example of the older and elders.
Exercise: Reader's Interpretation	

41. Krio Parebul	**bifo ɔt wata disgres na ɔg ia go kɔmɔt.**
Literal Translation	Before hot water is disgraced, it is hɔg's hair which will come out.

Interpretation	A great amount of effort is required to achieve success. Do whatever needs to be done to prevent failure.
Exercise:Reader's Interpretation	
42. Krio Parebul	**big man fɔ no usay fɔ it pan fɔl.**
Literal Translation	A big man should know which part should be eaten of the fowl.
Interpretation	An important person in society should choose to go the right way; know his/her status and how to comport him/herself.
Exercise: Reader's Interpretation	
43. Krio Parebul	**big man nɔ de was in an fɔ natin.**
Literal Translation	A big (important) man does not wash his hand for nothing.
Interpretation	An important man does not make preparations if there is nothing in store for him/if he does not stand to benefit.
Exercise: Reader's Interpretation	
44. Krio Parebul	**big man nɔ go de na tɔŋ kaw day na rop.**
Literal Translation	A big (important) man will not be in a town, a cow dies tied to a rope.

Interpretation	Influential personage will not be around and important things go undone, or good things go to waste.
Exercise: Reader's Interpretation	
45. Krio Parebul	**big wet kak we nɔ no insef, dɛn go dɔk am na bɔn pamayn.**
Literal Translation	A big white cock which does not know itself, they will dip it into burnt palmoil.
Interpretation	A person who does not behave in a way to earn the respect to which he is entitled, will find himself humiliated.
Exercise: Reader's Interpretation	
46. Krio Parebul	**big wɔd nɔ no se in masta po. (big mɔt nɔ no se....) (big tɔk nɔ no se...)**
Literal Translation	Big word does not know that its master is poor. (big mouth/big talk).
Interpretation	Boastful people not being aware that the wherewithal to back-up the boast is non-existent.
Exercise: Reader's Interpretation	
47. Krio Parebul	**bikɔs kɔtnos man de na tɔŋ, nain mek a nɔ fɔ se 'hɔn'.(nain mek a nɔ fɔ blo mi nos) (nain mek a nɔ fɔ sniz)**

16

Literal Translation	Because there is a cut-nosed (nose disfigured by wound) man here, is that why I shouldn't say, 'hn'. (is that why I shouldn't blow my nose?/sneeze)
Interpretation	Are you saying I shouldn't do or say something which can be construed as referring to the physical or mental state, or even a social scandal surrounding someone present here?
Exercise: Reader's Interpretation	
48. Krio Parebul	**bɔbɔ nɔ lɛk kol wata.**
Literal Translation	bɔbɔ (a kind of bean) does not like cold water.
Interpretation	Said of person, especially child, who constsntly merits severe corrective punishment/ a difficult person does not deserve lenient treatment.
Exercise: Reader's Interpretation	
49. Krio Parebul	**bɔd wan flay yu go shek tik.**
Literal Translation	The bird wants to fly you go and shake the tree.
Interpretation	Something is about to happen, you precipitate the event by your action.
Exercise: Reader's Interpretation	

50. Krio Parebul	bɔd we de go nɔ de luk wetin i de lɛf biɛn.
Literal Translation	A bird which is going does not look at what he is leaving behind.
Interpretation	Someone leaving e.g a job, house, country, political party etc etc, does not care about what is happening at the place left behind. Moving forward, you don't turn round to check.
Exercise: Reader's Interpretation	
51. Krio Parebul	bɔd we de it rɛs nɔ de mek nɔys.(....nɔ de tɔk)
Literal Translation	A bird which is eating rice does not make noise. (isn't noisy) (does not talk)
Interpretation	If one is benefitting from a situation, one doesn't brag.
Exercise: Reader's Interpretation	
52. Krio Parebul	broko kunu na waf sɛf gɛt ona. (broko kunu plɛnti na waf yu nɔ no uswan gɛt ona)
Literal Translation	Even a broken canoe at the wharf has an owner. (broken canoes are plenty at the wharf, you don't know which one has an owner.)

Interpretation	Do not violate or injure someone who appears weak or helpless, as you don't know which of the many seemingly helpless people will have help and support when the need arises.
Exercise: Reader's Interpretation	
53. Krio Parebul	**buk nɔ ba lay bɔt lay man kin rayt buk.**
Literal Translation	A book does not lie, but a man who tells lies can write a book.
Interpretation	The written wird is a good reference point as opposed to oral communication, but should not necessarily be accepted as gɔspɛl truth.
Exercise: Reader's Interpretation	
54. Krio Parebul	**chit nɔ de pan mɔndɔ. mɔndɔ na mɔndɔ.**
Literal Translation	There is no cheating when all eat together from the same bowl, using hands.
Interpretation	Injunction to be content with whatever falls to you in a distribution.
Exercise: Reader's Interpretation	

55. Krio Parebul	da ayɛn spun we se in wan chalenj mared krawo, na in mɔt go bɛn.
Literal Translation	That iron spoon which says it wants to challenge the crusty bits left at the bottom of the pot from rice cooked for a marriage (wedding), it is its mouth which will be bɛnt.
Interpretation	Insistence on doing what is beyond one's powers will result in one's getting hurt.
Exercise: Reader's Interpretation	
56. Krio Parebul	da bɛlɛ we bɔn tifman na in bɔn dɔkta. (......tifman na in bɔn rɛvrɛn)
Literal Translation	That belly which gave birth to a thief, is the one which gave birth to a doctor/reverend.
Interpretation	Similar backgrounds/origins can produce very dissimilar individuals.(very different exteriors can hide similar origins)/siblings can be different enough for one to be a rotten egg and the other an asset to society.
Exercise: Reader's Interpretation	
57. Krio Parebul	da blak got we yu nɔ kech santɛm na dak nɛt yu go kech am?

Literal Translation	That black goat which you haven't caught suntime (during the day) is it dark night you will catch it?
Interpretation	It is extremely unlikely that something which hasn't been done when conditions are favourable, will be executed at a less auspicious time.
Exercise: Reader's Interpretation	
58. Krio Parebul	**da briz we de disgres fɔl na biɛn am i de kɔmɔt.**
Literal Translation	That breeze which disgraces fowl, it is from behind it, it would come out (it comes from behind)
Interpretation	Be always vigilant, otherwise you might find yourself in big trouble without knowing why or how, or even being aware that anything was going wrong.
Exercise: Reader's Interpretation	
59. Krio Parebul	**da dabaru we dɛn dabaru ɔndafut we i nɔ gɛt ia, na di sem dabaru dɛn dabaru bitakola we i nɔ gɛ plit.**
Literal Translation	The curse (trickery) which made under the foot (sole of foot) not have hair, it is the same curse which made the bitter cola nut, not have a split.

Interpretation	The evil machinations which caused a certain condition, were also responsible for another type of condition.
Exercise: Reader's Interpretation	
60. Krio Parebul	**da dɔg we briŋ bon go kɛr bon.**
Literal Translation	The dɔg which brings a bone will carry (take away) a bone.
Interpretation	Beware of newsmongers. A newsbringer will be a newscarrier./Gossipers are two-way traffic – they bring and carry.
Exercise: Reader's Interpretation	
61. Krio Parebul	**da dɔg we swɛla big bon, i trɔs in baksay. (luk– na bikɔs babu biliv in baksay....)**
Literal Translation	The dog which swallows a big bone trusts its backside.(i.e that it will be able to excrete it)
Interpretation	Taking on a big challenge means absolute confidence in one's ability to cope.
Exercise: Reader's Interpretation	

62. Krio Parebul	da ed we kam fɔ tot ston, if yu put biba de i go fɔdɔm. (kɔmɔt)
Literal Translation	The head which comes to carry stone, if you put a beaver hat on it, it will fall off.
Interpretation	Destiny. An attempt made to thrust one who is destined to be lowly, into a position of power/ authority/ leadership, will not succeed. Pushed to a higher level, you'll come crashing down – to the level you were pre-destined to be.
Exercise: Reader's Interpretation	
63. Krio Parebul	da fɔl we fala yuba fɔ it sara rɛs na forod, na sup pɔt i go fɛn insɛf.
Literal Translation	The fowl which follows the vulture to eat sacrificial rice at the crossroads, will find itself inside the soup pot.
Interpretation	if you insist on going with someone else or going with the crowd to do what you are not experienced, trained, qualified, talented, or equipped to do, it will be catastrophic.
Exercise: Reader's Interpretation	

64. Krio Parebul	da gladi we de pan sapo nɔto in de pan krɔkrɔ.
Literal Translation	The happiness which is in sapo (sponge used for washing) is not the same which is in krokro. (krɔkrɔ – itching skin disease)
Interpretation	The perpetrator is happy, but the victim is not – conflicting interests.
Exercise: Reader's Interpretation	
65. Krio Parebul	da kak we wan kro bifo tɛm, na shit i go shit. (luk-pikin we wan wɛr in dadi trɔsis...)
Literal Translation	The cock which wants to crow before time (the appropriate time) will pass faeces. i.e while straining to do what it can't do.
Interpretation	A child who insists on doing something before maturity will not succeed, and will be extremely embarrassed.
Exercise: Reader's Interpretation	
66. Krio Parebul	da lay we yu go lay we go mek mared os nɔ skata, lay am. bɔt di tru we yu go tɔk we go skata mared os, nɔ tɔk am.(...lay we go mek mared os sidɔm...)

Literal Translation	The lie that you will lie which will make a marriage not break up, lie it. But the truth which you will talk which will break up a marriage, do not talk it.
Interpretation	It is acceptable to tell a lie to save a marriage, and inadvisable to speak a truth which will break up a marriage.
Exercise: Reader's Interpretation	
67. Krio Parebul	**da lif we swit na got mɔt, na in kin rɔn in bɛlɛ.**
Literal Translation	The leaf which is sweet in goat's mouth, it is it which runs its belly. (gives it diarrhoea)
Interpretation	What you most enjoy might be harmful to you. Do not overindulge.
Exercise: Reader's Interpretation	
68. Krio Parebul	**da mared we go swit, na frɔm di bachilɔz iv yu go no.**
Literal Translation	The marriage which will be sweet it is from the batchelor's eve you will know.
Interpretation	A good beginning is an indication of what is to come.
Exercise: Reader's Interpretation	

69. Krio Parebul	da pam-tri we mek frɛn wit pambɔd, na brum go lɛf na in ed.
Literal Translation	The palm tree which makes friends with a palm-bird, it is broom which will be left on its head.
Interpretation	You'll pay dearly if you make friends with people who have conflicting interests to yours.
Exercise: Reader's Interpretation	
70. Krio Parebul	da pamtri we wan fityay san, na brumtik go lɛf na in ed.
Literal Translation	The palm tree which wants to disrespect the sun, it is broom straw which will be left on its head.
Interpretation	Be careful how you relate to people who are powerful enough and are in a position to be able to hurt you. Annoying such people will be disasterous for you.
Exercise: Reader's Interpretation	
71. Krio Parebul	da pikin we se in go pul lɔŋ tit, na in go pul lip fɔ kɔba am.
Literal Translation	The child who says he will produce long teeth, it is he who will grow the lip to cover it.

Interpretation	One who deliberately does something out of the ordinary, will have the sole responsibility of ensuring that it works.
Exercise: Reader's Interpretation	
72. Krio Parebul	**da pikin we sɛ in nɔ wan lan buk, na kata go bi in ɛdmasta.**
Literal Translation	The child who says he/she does not want to learn book (be educated), it is kata which will be his/her headmaster. (Kata– a ring of cloth placed on the head, on top of which heavy loads are carried.)
Interpretation	A child who doesn't take his studies seriously will end up having only menial jobs.
Exercise: Reader's Interpretation	
73. Krio Parebul	**da ren we kam we mek bitas bita, na di sem ren kam we mek shugaken swit**
Literal Translation	The rain which came which made bitter leaves bitter, it is the same rain which came which made sugar cane sweet.
Interpretation	It is quite natural for people from the same environment and with the same background to be totally different.

Exercise: Reader's Interpretation	
74. Krio Parebul	da say we dɛn tay kaw, na de i go it gras.
Literal Translation	That place where they tie a cow, it is there it will eat grass.
Interpretation	One benefits from where one finds oneself.
Exercise: Reader's Interpretation	
75. Krio Parebul	da sem mɔt we ala 'ozana', na in de ala, 'krusifay!'
Literal Translation	That same mouth which shouted, 'Hosanna' is the one shouting, 'crusify'.
Interpretation	Human beings can be volatile.
Exercise: Reader's Interpretation	
76. Krio Parebul	da ship we briŋ Baybul, na in briŋ rɔm.
Literal Translation	The ship which brought the bible, is the one which brought rum.
Interpretation	Sometimes the same thing can be used for good or evil.
Exercise: Reader's Interpretation	
77. Krio Parebul	da siŋ we dɛn de siŋ na watasay, na in dɛn de briŋ na tɔŋ.

Literal Translation	The song which they sing at the stream, is the one they bring into the town.
Interpretation	This must have already been discussed somewhere else before it is being brought up here. What was a secret is now out in the open.
Exercise: Reader's Interpretation	
78. Krio Parebul	**da tik we man klem go ɔp, na im i go klem kam dɔŋ.**
Literal Translation	The tree which a man climbs to go up, is the one he will climb to come down.
Interpretation	Don't burn your bridges – you might need them for a return journey! i.e be careful how you treat people when you are in the ascendant; you don't know who you'll need when your luck changes.
Exercise: Reader's Interpretation	
79. Krio Parebul	**da tin we mek dɔg it bon, na di sem tin mek ɔg it pɔtɔpɔtɔ.**
Literal Translation	The thing which makes a dog eat bone, is the same thing which makes a hog eat mud.
Interpretation	Natural heredity traits as manifested in species. – can't be changed.

Exercise: Reader's Interpretation	
80. Krio Parebul	**dedebɔdi nɔ no ɔmɔs shrawd kɔs.**
Literal Translation	A dead body does not know how much a shroud costs.
Interpretation	Being completely oblivious to the state of affairs.
Exercise: Reader's Interpretation	
81. Krio Parebul	**dɛbul sɛf gɛt udat lɛk am.**
Literal Translation	Even a devil has who (someone who) likes him.
Interpretation	Everyone, no matter how negative his/her qualities, is liked by someone.
Exercise: Reader's Interpretation	
82. Krio Parebul	**dɛn de kɔnt yams bay dɔzin koko rol go de.**
Literal Translation	They are counting yams by dozen, cocoa rolls and goes there.
Interpretation	Said of person who tries to associate himself/herself with people of a higher Echelon, and far from being accepted, is ridiculed by that group.

Exercise: Reader's Interpretation	
83. Krio Parebul	**dɛn de tol yu bɛl yu de aks u day.**
Literal Translation	They are tolling your bell, you are asking, 'who died?'
Interpretation	They are talking about you in your presence and you do not realize that you are the subject of discussion.
Exercise: Reader's Interpretation	
84. Krio Parebul	**dɛn gi am rum i want pala. (dɛn gi yu rum yu aks fɔ pala.)**
Literal Translation	They give him a room, he wants the parlour.
Interpretation	Instead of being grateful for a favour done for you, you are demanding more.
Exercise: Reader's Interpretation	
85. Krio Parebul	**dɛn nɔ de bay ɔg fɔ in vɔys.**
Literal Translation	They do not buy a hog for its voice.
Interpretation	Certain goods are not bought for obvious attributes, which might not be attractive, but for their utility and intrinsic value.
Exercise: Reader's Interpretation	

86. Krio Parebul	dɛn se med in Inglan yu se jigida.
Literal Translation	They say, 'made in England', you say jigida. (small cheap ornamental beads)
Interpretation	The discussion is about quality goods, you refer to things of little worth
Exercise: Reader's Interpretation	
87. Krio Parebul	dɛn se mɔreman bɔn yu aks fɔ in biabia.(dɛn se karamɔkɔ bɔn yu se we in bia?
Literal Translation	They say a muslim diviner is burnt, you ask for his beard.
Interpretation	There has been a tragic accident, and you are asking about a triviality which should not even be considered in the circumstances.
Exercise: Reader's Interpretation	
88. Krio Parebul	dɛn se u wɔwɔ go gɛt wata babu bɔs kray.
Literal Translation	They say who is ugly go and get water, the babu bursts out crying.(bursts into tears)
Interpretation	Someone understands and responds to an overt hint directed at him/her.

Exercise: Reader's Interpretation	
89. Krio Parebul	**dɛn se vɛks tek nɔ vɛks lɛf.**
Literal Translation	They say vex and take, don't be vexed and leave. (i.e. and not take.)
Interpretation	Do not lose out on something proffered because you are angry or upset. Accept what is on offer even though you are not pleased about it.
Exercise: Reader's Interpretation	
90. *Krio* Parebul	**dɛn sɛn mɔnki, mɔnki sɛn in tel.**
Literal Translation	They send the monkey, the monkey sends its tail.
Interpretation	Delegating a request for one to do something, to one's subordinate.
Exercise: Reader's Interpretation	
91. Krio Parebul	**dɛn tot yu na bak yu nɔ no se rod fa.**
Literal Translation	They are carrying you on the back, you do not know that the road is far. (that it's a long journey)
Interpretation	Not being sufficiently appreciative because one is unaware of the magnitude of the help being given.

Exercise: Reader's Interpretation	
92. Krio Parebul	**dɛn tot yu na bak yu se rod fa.**
Literal Translation	They are carrying you on the back, you say the road is far. (the road is long)
Interpretation	Complaining in spite of all the help being given.
Exercise: Reader's Interpretation	
93. Krio Parebul	**di dɛbul we yu sabi bɛtɛ pas di enjɛl we yu nɔ no**
Literal Translation	The dɛvil whom you know is better than the angel whom you do not know.
Interpretation	It is advisable to put up with who you already know, and are used to interacting with. Someone else whom you don't know, but who seems a much better proposition, might turn out to be not what you expected.
Exercise: Reader's Interpretation	
94. Krio Parebul	**dɔg de fɛt/rɔn fɔ in layf, lɛpɛt de fɛt/rɔn fɔ in karakta.(fɔ in gud nem)**
Literal Translation	The dog is fighting/running for its life, the leopard is fighting/running for its character.

Interpretation	The outcome of a matter affects the very existence of one party, but not so catastrophic for the other. Having completely different agenda and opposing priorities. e.g the man in the street striving to make ends meet, while the higher echelons striving to maintain their position in society.
Exercise: Reader's Interpretation	
95. Krio Parebul	**dɔg drim day na in bɛlɛ. (....lɛf na in bɛlɛ**
Literal Translation	Dog's dream dies in its belly.
Interpretation	One keeps one's secrets to oneself.
Exercise: Reader's Interpretation	
96. Krio Parebul	**dɔg kres te, i no faya.**
Literal Translation	No matter how crazy a dɔg is, it knows fire.
Interpretation	No matter how disorientated you may be, be it due to madness, drunkenness, grief etc, there are certain dangerous situations in which your brain will function well enough to interpret the danger correctly.
Exercise: Reader's Interpretation	

97. Krio Parebul	dɔg na dɔg.
Literal Translation	A dog is a dog.
Interpretation	A contemptible person does not change.
Exercise: Reader's Interpretation	
98. Krio Parebul	dɔks nɔ de kupe bɔt in wes de shek.
Literal Translation	The duck does not wear a bustle, but its hips shake.(sway)
Interpretation	One does not need to have the designated tool or attribute inorder to be able to produce a desired result.
Exercise: Reader's Interpretation	
99. Krio Parebul	dɔti wata sɛf kin ɔt faya.
Literal Translation	Even dirty water can put out a fire.
Interpretation	Even a tool which is not in the best condition might do the job effectively./Even something regarded as useless, might prove useful.
Exercise: Reader's Interpretation	
100. Krio Parebul	dray dɔg swit fɔ it bɔt wetin fɔ it te dɔg dray.
Literal Translation	Dried dog is sweet to eat, but what to eat until the dog is dried?

Interpretation	A later outcome may prove to be better, but the need is now.
Exercise: Reader's Interpretation	
101. Krio Parebul	**ekuru dɔg na in kin kil lɛpɛt.**
Literal Translation	A mangy dog is the one which can kill a leopard.
Interpretation	A seemingly helpless person can succeed in accomplishing surprising feats. The apparently weak and helpless can be the ruin of the strong.
Exercise: Reader's Interpretation	
102. Krio Parebul	**enjɛl nɔ ba fityay God.**
Literal Translation	An angel does not disrespect God.
Interpretation	Said of one who has suffered dire consequencies as a result of exhibiting unwarranted rudeness to, or unjustifiably challenging, a much more powerful person or persons.
Exercise: Reader's Interpretation	
103. Krio Parebul	**Estin drink Watalo drɔnk.**
Literal Translation	Hastings drink, Watalo gets drunk.
Interpretation	Suffering the ill effects of another person's actions.

Exercise: Reader's Interpretation	
104. Krio Parebul	**ɛlifant ed nɔto pikin lod.**
Literal Translation	The elephant's head is not a child's load.
Interpretation	That problem is much too big for one not very competent to cope with.
Exercise: Reader's Interpretation	
105. Krio Parebul	**ɛmti bag nɔ ba tinap.**
Literal Translation	An empty bag does not stand up.
Interpretation	One cannot function effectively on an empty stomach. You cannot work effectively if you are not properly equipped.
Exercise: Reader's Interpretation	
106. Krio Parebul	**ɛni gyal pikin we wan put yay na trit, wɛn trit bɛt am, i go tek in big to krach in yes. (luk– trit nɔ gɛ tit bɔt i de bɛt.)**
Literal Translation	Any girl child who wants to put her eyes on the street, when the street bites her, she will take her big toe to scratch her ear.

Interpretation	Any girl who is always out of the house, presumably with undesirable company, exhibiting anti-social behaviour, will find herself in a predicament, from which she will do absolutely anything to extricate herself, and will then regret her wanton behavior.
Exercise: Reader's Interpretation	
107. Krio Parebul	**ɛp mi kɔnt kɔpɔ nɔ min na yu yon.**
Literal Translation	Help me to count coppers does not mean it is yours. (coppers– coins made from copper – now, money in general)
Interpretation	A reminder that you have no say in this matter; no rights in the proceedings, you are merely a helper.
Exercise: Reader's Interpretation	
108. Krio Parebul	**ɛvride nɔto krismɛs.**
Literal Translation	Everyday is not Christmas.
Interpretation	Life can't be wonderful all the time. There are good times and bad times.
Exercise: Reader's Interpretation	

109. Krio Parebul	fambul sofut na in nɔmɔ de jomp fambul yayam.(na os sofut de jomp os yayam.
Literal Translation	Only a relative will jump over a relative's food with a foot which has a nasty Sore.
Interpretation	People will put up with intolerable behaviour only from relatives; or intolerable situations only because of relatives.
Exercise: Reader's Interpretation	
110. Krio Parebul	fambul tik kin bɛn bɔt i nɔ ba brok.
Literal Translation	The family tree may bend but it does not break.
Interpretation	Rifts will occur in families, but the relationships will never be completely severed.
Exercise: Reader's Interpretation	
111. Krio Parebul	fawe kɔtintri gud fɔ luk.(luk– fawe kɔtintri nɔ gɛt....)
Literal Translation	A far–away cotton tree is good to look at.
Interpretation	Something which is far away from you looks good because you cannot see its flaws.

Exercise: Reader's Interpretation	
112. Krio Parebul	**fawe kɔtintri nɔ gɛt chukchuk. (luk–fawe kɔtintri gud....)**
Literal Translation	A far–away cotton tree does not have thorns.
Interpretation	You can't see the negative aspect of something which is far away.
Exercise: Reader's Interpretation	
113. Krio Parebul	**fayn wan nɔ de pan babu.**
Literal Translation	Fine ones do not exist among baboons.(fine – beautiful)
Interpretation	No one is better than the other; they are all the same. Six of one and half a dozen of the other.
Exercise: Reader's Interpretation	
114. Krio Parebul	**fish it fish uswan na sɔlwata yon de?**
Literal Translation	Fish eats fish, what has that got to do with salt water. (the ocean)
Interpretation	They are kinsmen, so no matter how much you see and disapprove of what they do to each other, it's none of your business.

Exercise: Reader's Interpretation	
115. Krio Parebul	**fish nɔ de drawn na wata. (mina nɔ ba drawn na oshɔn.)**
Literal Translation	Fish does not drown in water.
Interpretation	One knows how to survive in one's own environment.
Exercise: Reader's Interpretation	
116. Krio Parebul	**fishuman nɔ ba se in fish rɔtin.**
Literal Translation	A fishwoman does not say her fish is rotten.
Interpretation	One would never admit that one's goods are substandard, or admit to flaws in something one has done.
Exercise: Reader's Interpretation	
117. Krio Parebul	**fɔ mas agidi fɔ lɛpɛt nɔto di tin, na udat fɔ gi am.**
Literal Translation	To mash agidi for a leopard is not the thing, it is who to give him.(agidi– food made of boiled ground corn.
Interpretation	Who will be brave enough to carry out this dangerous act? /who will bell the cat?
Exercise: Reader's Interpretation	

118. Krio Parebul	fɔdɔm fɔ mi, a fɔdɔm fɔ yu. (luk– rɔb mi bak a rɔb yu yon.)
Literal Translation	Fall down for me, I fall down for you.
Interpretation	If you seek my interest I shall seek yours.
Exercise: Reader's Interpretation	
119. Krio Parebul	fɔl fɔ sɛl, kɛnɛri fɔ ɛng na kej.
Literal Translation	Fowl to sell. Canary to hang in cage.
Interpretation	Reffering to persons pursuing different lifestyles and awaiting opposing fetes because of inherent differences.
Exercise: Reader's Interpretation	
120. Krio Parebul	fɔl wan wisul bɔt i nɔ gɛ jabon.
Literal Translation	Fowl wants to whistle, but it does not have a jaw bone.
Interpretation	Incapable of pursuing a particular dream because you are deficient in a required attribute.
Exercise: Reader's Interpretation	
121. Krio Parebul	fɔl we nɔ yɛri 'shi', go yɛri ston. (da fɔl we nɔ yeri 'shi'.....)
Literal Translation	The fowl which does not hear 'shoo' will hear stone.

Interpretation	One who does not respond to gentle warnings, will respond to harsh treatment.
Exercise: Reader's Interpretation	
122. Krio Parebul	**fɔs ful na ful, sɛkɛn ful na dam ful. (....sɛkɛn ful na bikful)**
Literal Translation	A fool the first time is a fool, a fool the second time is a damn fool.
Interpretation	A man who makes the same mistake more than once is indeed stupid.
Exercise: Reader's Interpretation	
123. Krio Parebul	**fɔseka fish yu go it tumbu.**
Literal Translation	Because of fish, you'll eat maggots.
Interpretation	You'll do disagreeable things inorder to get what you want.
Exercise: Reader's Interpretation	
124. Krio Parebul	**fɔseka pikin nain mek kombra sɛt yay bɛt fatfut.**
Literal Translation	Because of a child that is why a mother shut her eyes and bit a millipede.

Interpretation	A mother will do extremely unpleasant things for the good of her child. Do what you wouldn't readily have done to get what you want.
Exercise: Reader's Interpretation	
125. Krio Parebul	**fri po bɛtɛ pas tayt jɛntri.**
Literal Translation	Free poor is better than tight wealth
Interpretation	It is better to be poor and free to live your life the way you want, than to have a lot of money and not be able to do so.
Exercise: Reader's Interpretation	
126. Krio Parebul	**fufu nɔ de fityay ɔkrɔ sup. (drɔsup – luk 37)**
Literal Translation	Fufu is not disrespectful to okra sup. (fufu– made from fermented cassava)
Interpretation	You cannot be disrespectful to someone who helps to make life easy for you.
Exercise: Reader's Interpretation	
127. Krio Parebul	**gɛt gɛt nɔ want, want want nɔ gɛt.**
Literal Translation	Get get does not want. want want does not get.

Interpretation	Those who have, don't appreciate. Those who want, don't have. The grass is always greener on the other side.
Exercise: Reader's Interpretation	
128. Krio Parebul	**got de swɛt, na ia kɔba (r) am. (got sɛf de swɛt......)**
Literal Translation	A goat sweats, it is hair covers it. (even a goat sweats)
Interpretation	People usually conceal their troubles.
Exercise: Reader's Interpretation	
129. Krio Parebul	**got ed ɛn ship ed nɔto wan.**
Literal Translation	A goat's head and a ship's head are not the same.
Interpretation	People's fate differ.
Exercise: Reader's Interpretation	
130. Krio Parebul	**got ɛn ship nɔ de mit na wan viranda. (luk – na ren mek...)**
Literal Translation	Goats and sheep do not meet in the same veranda.
Interpretation	People who are not on the same rung of the socio- economic ladder do not fraternize. Their paths don't cross.

Exercise: Reader's Interpretation	
131. Krio Parebul	**got kaka wan rol yu go kik am. (....yu go tek brum swip am) (luk– bɔd wan flay yu go shek tik)(oluman wan day yu go tek tik wap am)**
Literal Translation	The goat's faeces want to roll, yu go and kick it.
Interpretation	Something is about to happen, you precipitate the event by your action.
Exercise: Reader's Interpretation	
132. Krio Parebul	**got we na yu gɛt fɔ tot, nɔ sidɔm i ledɔm na pɔtɔpɔtɔ.**
Literal Translation	A goat which it is you have to carry, don't sit down (and let) it lie down in mud.
Interpretation	Don't act as if you don't care about something which is going to affect you. Make your own input.
Exercise: Reader's Interpretation	
133. Krio Parebul	**Gɔd gari mɔs swɛl.**
Literal Translation	God's gari must swell.

Interpretation	Commenting on the futility of attemptting to conceal a pregnancy; that it will be seen sooner or later. It will 'swell'.
Exercise: Reader's Interpretation	
134. Krio Parebul	**Gɔd pas kɔnsibul.**
Literal Translation	God is more than a constable.
Interpretation	God is more powerful than anything or anyone, including the police, and intervenes in favour of the weak and disadvantaged.
Exercise: Reader's Interpretation	
135. Krio Parebul	**gud neba bɛtɛ pas fawe fambul.**
Literal Translation	A good neighbour is better than a far-away relative.
Interpretation	Having someone near at hand is much better than having to rely on Someone much farther away, even though the latter might be the preferred choice.
Exercise: Reader's Interpretation	
136. Krio Parebul	**gud trik bɛtɛ pas fayn pafyum.**
Literal Translation	Good habits are better than fine perfume.(sweet smelling perfume)

Interpretation	Having good habits are much more desirable than appearance or outward presentation.
Exercise: Reader's Interpretation	
137. Krio Parebul	**gud wɔd pul kola.**
Literal Translation	Good word pulls out colanut. (colanut is ceremonially valued)
Interpretation	It is easier to get what you want if you Know how to say the right things.
Exercise: Reader's Interpretation	
138. Krio Parebul	**i smɛl bifo i rɔtin.**
Literal Translation	It smells before it rots.
Interpretation	Situations don't deteriorate suddenly; there are usually signs. Things get worse by degrees.
Exercise: Reader's Interpretation	
139. Krio Parebul	**if ayɛnpɔt kray kol, wetin kɔntripɔt fɔ se?**
Literal Translation	If the iron pot cries that it is cold, what should the country pot say? (kɔntripɔt- earthenware pot)

Interpretation	If the fairly comfortable ones feel the pinch, how much more the less fortunate? If the ones who are in a better position to cope with a difficult situation are not finding it easy, what can the less capable do?
Exercise: Reader's Interpretation	
140. Krio Parebul	**if briz nɔ blo wata nɔ go shek.**
Literal Translation	If the breeze does not blow, the water will not shake.
Interpretation	This would not have happened if something hadn't caused it to happen, so it's no use refusing to face up to the fact that something did happen.
Exercise: Reader's Interpretation	
141. Krio Parebul	**if lɔs bɔs pan lɛm wetin fɔ tek mɛn krɔkrɔ?**
Literal Translation	If lice appear on limes, what should be taken to heal krɔkrɔ? (krɔkrɔ– luk 64)
Interpretation	You are really in trouble because what you are relying on to solve your problem, itself has a problem.
Exercise: Reader's Interpretation	

142. Krio Parebul	if lɔs nɔ dɔn na ed blɔd nɔ go dɔn na finga.
Literal Translation	As long as there are lice on the head, there will be blood on the finger.
Interpretation	As long as this problem exists, these ill effects will continue to recur.
Exercise: Reader's Interpretation	
143. Krio Parebul	if os nɔ sɛl yu trit nɔ go bay yu.
Literal Translation	If the house does not sell you the street will not buy you.
Interpretation	Suffering the consequencies of betrayal by close friends or family members. If your own home does not betray you, outsiders will not have the chance to harm you.
Exercise: Reader's Interpretation	
144. Krio Parebul	if ɔlman put in trɔbul na fɛnch, yu go rɔn go tek yu yon.
Literal Translation	If everyone puts their troubles on a fence, you will run and go and take your own.
Interpretation	If you knew other people's problems, you will realize how much better off you are.
Exercise: Reader's Interpretation	

145. Krio Parebul	if pɛpɛ swit, rɔb am na yu sofut.
Literal Translation	If pepper is sweet, rub it on the sore on your foot.
Interpretation	If it's good enough for me, it's good enough for you. If you're offering me, you first try it / also a counselling against the misuse of pepper.
Exercise: Reader's Interpretation	
146. Krio Parebul	if yes nɔ yɛri, at nɔ go vɛks.
Literal Translation	If the ear doesn't hear, the heart will not be vexed.
Interpretation	You can't be upset about what you don't know.
Exercise: Reader's Interpretation	
147. Krio Parebul	if yu fala babu fɔ in wɔwɔ, yu go bit am te yu kil am.
Literal Translation	If you allow the baboon's ugliness to get to you, you will beat it until you kill it.
Interpretation	There are some aspects of people you can't change, no matter what you do, if what you want to change is an intrinsic part of them.
Exercise: Reader's Interpretation	

148. Krio Parebul	if yu gɛ natay yu go fray ston.(natay-oil made from crushed palm kernel nut).
Literal Translation	If you have nut-oil you'll fry a stone.
Interpretation	You are so enterprising that if you have the basics, you'll attempt anything at all, even the seemingly impossible – you are unstoppable.
Exercise: Reader's Interpretation	
149. Krio Parebul	if yu koko ros, sidɔm na kɔna it am saful.
Literal Translation	If your coco-yam is roasted, sit down in a corner and eat it quietly.
Interpretation	Don't brag about your good fortune.
Exercise: Reader's Interpretation	
150. Krio Parebul	if yu lɛk mɔnki yu gɛ fɔ lɛk in blakan. (........lɛk in tel)
Literal Translation	If you like the monkey, you have to like its black hand. (...like its tail)
Interpretation	You should accept the negative qualities of someone you like.
Exercise: Reader's Interpretation	
151. Krio Parebul	if yu luk bɔtɔm kɔntripɔt yu nɔ go drink. (kɔntripɔt–luk 139)

Literal Translation	If you look at the bottom of a country pot, you won't drink.
Interpretation	If you want to take all the hazards into consideration, you won't do anything.
Exercise: Reader's Interpretation	
152. Krio Parebul	**if yu mek yusɛf ɔni di wɔl go lik yu.**
Literal Translation	If you make yourself honey the world will lick you.
Interpretation	If you are very weak and accommodating, people will take undue advantage over you/exploit you with impunity.
Exercise: Reader's Interpretation	
153. Krio Parebul	**if yu no se yu nɔ gɛ fut, we dɛn se fɔ go jɔni, yu go go bifo.**
Literal Translation	If you know that you do not have feet, when they say to go on a journey, you will go before. (go ahead)
Interpretation	If you know you have a weakness, you should do something to compensate for It.
Exercise: Reader's Interpretation	
154. Krio Parebul	**if yu nɔ lɛk mɔnki yu nɔ go lɛk in tel.**
Literal Translation	If you do not like the monkey, you will not like its tail.

Interpretation	If, for whatever reason, you do not like someone, you probably will not like his/her children or even that person's close associates.
Exercise: Reader's Interpretation	
155. Krio Parebul	**if yu nɔ no usay yu de go, no usay yu kɔmɔt.**
Literal Translation	If you do not know where you are going, know where you come from.
Interpretation	Your life may not be what you want it to be right now but don't forget your background and the morals and ethics of your culture. Knowing who you are and comporting yourself admirably just might help you to get to where you want to go.
Exercise: Reader's Interpretation	
156. Krio Parebul	**if yu nɔ want mɔnki tel fɔ tɔch yu, nɔ jɔyn mɔnki dans.(luk– shɔtat man..)**
Literal Translation	If you do not want the monkey's tail to touch you, do not join the monkey dance.

Interpretation	If you don't want to be made uncomfortable by the behaviour of people who are not on the same wavelength as you, then don't interact too intimately with them.
Exercise: Reader's Interpretation	
157. Krio Parebul	**if yu nɔ wan si yu mɔdɛnlɔ in rɛd mɔt nɔ gi am rɛd banga.**
Literal Translation	If you do not want to see your mother in law's red mouth do not give her red palm kernel.
Interpretation	If you don't want someone to whom you are in some way beholden, venting their anger at you, then do not deliberately do something to provoke. Don't do things that will upset or embarrass you later.
Exercise: Reader's Interpretation	
158. Krio Parebul	**if yu ple wit dɔg tumɔs i go wan lik yu mɔt.**
Literal Translation	If you play with a dog too much, it will want to lick your mouth.
Interpretation	'Familiarity breeds contempt.'

Exercise: Reader's Interpretation	
159. Krio Parebul	**if yu sabi fɔ ple wit lɛpɛt yu go sɔk in bɔbi.**
Literal Translation	If you know how to play with a leopard, you will suck its breasts.
Interpretation	If you study someone closely, and handle them the right way, you will be able to get even a very powerful or dangerous person to do exactly what you want them to do, without their realizing it.
Exercise: Reader's Interpretation	
160. Krio Parebul	**if yu wan si yu got de bɔn twin, yu gɛt fɔ de de yusɛf.**
Literal Translation	If you want to see your goat giving birth to twins, you have to be there yourself.
Interpretation	If you want to be sure that something important which affects you goes well, especially in business ventures, do it youself, or at least be there to supervise the process; be a part of it.
Exercise: Reader's Interpretation	

161. Krio Parebul	if yu wan tredin pus yu fɔ gɛt kɔba blay.
Literal Translation	If you want to trade pussy cats, you should have a basket with a cover.
Interpretation	If you want to do something, you should have everything necessary to ensure that whatever it is, gets successfully executed.
Exercise: Reader's Interpretation	
162. Krio Parebul	if yu yams wayt, kɔba (r) am.
Literal Translation	If your yam is white, cover it.(if yu koko ros, sidɔm na kɔna it am saful)
Interpretation	Don't boast about your good fortune. Don't show-off.
Exercise: Reader's Interpretation	
163. Krio Parebul	int no in masta, kabaslɔt no in misis.
Literal Translation	Hint knows its master, kabaslot knows its mistress. (kabaslɔt –traditional long print dress worn by middle-aged and elderly Krio women)
Interpretation	They are talking about you in your presence with hints couched such that you know what they are referring to, and they know you know.

58

Exercise: Reader's Interpretation	
164. Krio Parebul	**jɛlɔs krab nɔ ba fat.**
Literal Translation	A jealous crab does not get fat.
Interpretation	Jealousy is not conducive to happiness.
Exercise: Reader's Interpretation	
165. Krio Parebul	**jɛntri nɔ kam bay takiti.**
Literal Translation	Wealth does not come by undue frenetic activity.
Interpretation	You cannot get wealthy overnight, but by slow assiduous work.
Exercise: Reader's Interpretation	
166. Krio Parebul	**Jɔn bad–ed go na jakato fam i mit ɔl dɔn rɛp. (......ɔl dɔn yala)**
Literal Translation	John bad–head goes to a jakato farm, he meets all have ripened.
Interpretation	Jakato rots vey quickly, so someone dogged by bad luck, would meet a field of rotten fruit. Comment about someone who, more often than not, has bad luck.

Exercise: Reader's Interpretation	
167. Krio Parebul	**Jɔn pamayn trowe na Jɔn rɛs.**
Literal Translation	John's palmoil spilt on John's rice.
Interpretation	One does something which backfires on someone very close or at oneself. Internal affair, so there should be no interference.
Exercise: Reader's Interpretation	
168. Krio Parebul	**kaka nɔ de drɛb kaka na grasfil.**
Literal Translation	Faeces will not drive faeces from a grass field.
Interpretation	We are both exactly the same type, or, at exactly the same level, so we have equal rights here.
Exercise: Reader's Interpretation	
169. Krio Parebul	**Kaka nɔ gɛ chukchuk bɔt we yu mas am yu go jomp.**
Literal Translation	Faeces don't have thorns, but when you tread on them, you will jump.

Interpretation	A seemingly harmless situation can prove quite unpleasant./ Someone who does not seem to possess forceful attributes might be capable of producing as unpalatable results as a stronger personality.
Exercise: Reader's Interpretation	
170. Krio Parebul	**kaki nɔ du fɔ steshɔn masta, pɔta se i wan lɔŋ panks.**
Literal Translation	Khaki is not enough for station master, the porter says he wants long trousers.
Interpretation	There isn't enough of this for the leaders, yet the workers have the impudence to ask for more than their superiors have.
Exercise: Reader's Interpretation	
171. Krio Parebul	**kakroch nɔ gɛ pawa na fɔl kɔntri.**
Literal Translation	The cockroach does not have power in fowl country.
Interpretation	You can't have any influence in hostile territory.
Exercise: Reader's Interpretation	

172. Krio Parebul	kanda nɔ du fɔ drɔma, yu se fɔ kɔt af gi yu.
Literal Translation	The skin is not enough for the drum, you say to cut half and give you.
Interpretation	A retort to someone who is asking to be given some of what you have, when you don't even have enough for your own needs.
Exercise: Reader's Interpretation	
173. Krio Parebul	kapu sɛns nɔ kapu wɔd.
Literal Translation	Grab sense, don't grab words.
Interpretation	Listen carefully, and try to learn from what you hear, instead of just regarding everything you hear as idle chatter. Look at the bigger picture.
Exercise: Reader's Interpretation	
174. Krio Parebul	kaw day usay nɛf nɔ de. (kaw day da say we nɛf nɔ de)
Literal Translation	A cow dies where there is no knife.
Interpretation	An opportunity arises at a place where, or a time when, one does not have the wherewithal to take advantage of it.
Exercise: Reader's Interpretation	

175. Krio Parebul	kaw ed gɛt ɔn, naim mek i nɔ de tot drɔm.
Literal Translation	A cow's head has horns, that is why it doesn't carry drums.
Interpretation	One is not equipped to be able to carry out a particular exercise.
Exercise: Reader's Interpretation	
176. *Krio* Parebul	kaw ol te, in liba nɔ ol.
Literal Translation	No matter how old a cow is, its liver is not old.
Interpretation	Referring to, or said by, an older person who is seemingly acting younger than is the norm . Also has sexual innuendos.
Exercise: Reader's Interpretation	
177. Krio Parebul	kaw we nɔ gɛ tel, na Gɔd go drɛb in flay.
Literal Translation	A cow which hasn't got a tail, it is God who will drive away its flies.
Interpretation	It is God who helps the helpless.
Exercise: Reader's Interpretation	

178. Krio Parebul	kaw we se i wan pwɛl rod, na in wes go fil am. (da kaw we se i wan dɔti trit, na in wes go fil am) (kaw se in de pwɛl rod, i nɔ no se na in baksay i de pwɛl)
Literal Translation	The cow that says it wants to spoil the road, it is its bottom which will feel it.
Interpretation	In the process of doing something to hurt someone else, you hurt yourself more.
Exercise: Reader's Interpretation	
179. Krio Parebul	kes trɔŋ sote, na mɔt go tɔk am.
Literal Translation	No matter how difficult the case, it is mouth which will talk it.
Interpretation	No problem is too difficult to be resolved through discussion and negotiation.
Exercise: Reader's Interpretation	
180. Krio Parebul	kɛr Gladi go na trit, lɛf Sɔro na os.
Literal Translation	Take happiness to go into the street, leave Sorrow at home.
Interpretation	Show joy to the outside world, leave sorrow at home.
Exercise: Reader's Interpretation	

181. Krio Parebul	kil babu sho mɔnki.
Literal Translation	Kill the baboon and show it to the monkey.
Interpretation	Overdress/go to town/dress to kill.
Exercise: Reader's Interpretation	

182. Krio Parebul	kil dɔg bifo dɔg yay lɛ dɔg no se day de.
Literal Translation	Kill a dog before a dog's eye so that dogs know that death exists.
Interpretation	Take drastic measures in full view of members of a group, so that they will realize you absolutely mean to do anything you say you'll do, and that you will stop at nothing to gain your ends.
Exercise: Reader's Interpretation	

183. Krio Parebul	kip tik biɛn do fɔ we yu neba go kres.
Literal Translation	Keep a stick behind a door for when your neighbour goes crazy.
Interpretation	Prepare for self-preservation in case of emergencies. Always have a plan B.
Exercise: Reader's Interpretation	

184. Krio Parebul	Kol kech dɔg te i nɔ go wam insɛf na lɛpɛt kanda.
Literal Translation	No matter how cold a dog is, it will not warm itself on a leopard's skin.
Interpretation	It does not matter in what straits people find themselves, they know, or should know, how far they can dare.
Exercise: Reader's Interpretation	
185. Krio Parebul	kombra fɔl nɔ de jomp faya.
Literal Translation	A mother hen does not jump over fire.
Interpretation	when you have children you should be very careful what you do, lest they copy you and get hurt.
Exercise: Reader's Interpretation	
186. Krio Parebul	kɔmiɛl nɔ gɛ bɔks bɔt i de chenj.
Literal Translation	The chameleon does not have a box, but it changes.(clothes)
Interpretation	Don't judge by what meets the eye.
Exercise: Reader's Interpretation	
187. Krio Parebul	kɔniman day kɔniman bɛr am.
Literal Translation	A cunning man dies, a cunning man buries him.
Interpretation	However tricky a man may be, there is always someone as cunning or even more cunning than him.

Exercise: Reader's Interpretation	
188. Krio Parebul	**kɔtintri fɔdɔm sote, i ay pas gras.**
Literal Translation	No matter how flat a cotton tree falls, it is taller than grass.
Interpretation	A great man, however reduced, is superior to nonentity.
Exercise: Reader's Interpretation	
189. Krio Parebul	**kɔtnos man nɔ de tot pɛpɛbag.**
Literal Translation	A cut-nosed man does not carry a sack used as a container for pepper. (kɔtnos – luk 47)
Interpretation	If you have a weakness, you do not leave yourself open to something which will adversely affect that weakness.
Exercise: Reader's Interpretation	
190. Krio Parebul	**kres kin mɛn bɔt ful nɔ ba mɛn.**
Literal Translation	Craziness can be cured, but stupidity cannot be cured.
Interpretation	Bemoaning the fact that there is no cure for being a fool.

Exercise: Reader's Interpretation	
191. Krio Parebul	**kresman kres te, i nɔ go tek bled wep in wes.**
Literal Translation	No matter how crazy a madman is, he will not take a blade to wipe his bottom.
Interpretation	No matter how enraged or disorientated a person might be, he will know where to draw the line in his actions, and will not do anything which will seriously harm or destroy him.
Exercise: Reader's Interpretation	
192. Krio Parebul	**krio sup na in fɔ tek it krio rɛs.**
Literal Translation	Krio soup is what should be taken to eat Krio rice.
Interpretation	Only one who is knowledgeable about the subject will be able to handle a problem arising in that area.
Exercise: Reader's Interpretation	
193. Krio Parebul	**Krio tikpun du fɔ tɔn Krio rɛs. (Krio tikpun na in fɔ tek tɔn Krio sup pɔt.)**
Literal Translation	Krio wooden spoon is enough to turn Krio rice.

Interpretation	A Krio man understands how to deal with a fellow Krio.
Exercise:Reader's Interpretation	
194. Krio Parebul	**krɔkrɔ nɔ de slev fɔ yɔs.**
Literal Translation	krɔkrɔ is not a slave for yaws. (krɔkrɔ – luk 64)
Interpretation	The one is not a servant to the other. They are both at the same level.
Exercise: Reader's Interpretation	
195. Krio Parebul	**lɛf kanda gi drɔma.**
Literal Translation	Leave the skin for the drum/drummer.
Interpretation	Leave the experts to do their job.
Exercise: Reader's Interpretation	
196. Krio Parebul	**lɛf plasas fɔ dray rɛs.**
Literal Translation	Leave palaver sauce for dry rice. (dry rice – rice with no sauce on it)
Interpretation	Let's not talk any more about this. We'll discuss later, at a more appropriate time.
Exercise: Reader's Interpretation	
197. Krio Parebul	**lɔŋ rod nɔ kil nɔbɔdi.**
Literal Translation	A long road does not kill anybody.

Interpretation	As long as you achieve your objective, it doesn't matter how long you take to do it.
Exercise: Reader's Interpretation	
198. Krio Parebul	**lubi nɔto slev na ɔkrɔ sup.**
Literal Translation	Lubi is not a slave in okra sup.
Interpretation	I don't have to do this you know, I'm just doing a favour.
Exercise: Reader's Interpretation	
199. Krio Parebul	**mami nɔ ba bɛt in pikin rich di bon.**
Literal Translation	A mother does not bite her child to reach down to the bone.
Interpretation	A mother's punishment to her child is always softened by love, so she will never go to unbearable lengths.
Exercise: Reader's Interpretation	
200. Krio Parebul	**man liv bay man.**
Literal Translation	Man lives by man.
Interpretation	No man is an island.
Exercise: Reader's Interpretation	
201. Krio Parebul	**Man nɔ de kɔmɔt na os go na do we ren de kam.**
Literal Translation	A Man does not come out of a house to go outside when rain is coming.

Interpretation	You don't leave a comfortable situation for a less agreeable one. / You don't walk from safety into trouble.
Exercise: Reader's Interpretation	
202. Krio Parebul	**man ɔs na in de bia kik. (man jakas naim de tot lod)**
Literal Translation	A male horse is the one which can bear kicks.
Interpretation	One who claims to be strong should be prepared to face tough situations.
Exercise: Reader's Interpretation	'
203. Krio Parebul	**man we bɔn in biabia, na in fɔs go fil am.**
Literal Translation	A man who burns his beard, it is he first will feel it.
Interpretation	He who makes a mistake will be the first to suffer the consequences.
Exercise: Reader's Interpretation	
204. Krio Parebul	**man we wan gɛ bɛlɛ, na bɛringrɔn i go bɔn.**
Literal Translation	A man who wants to get pregnant, it is in the cemetery he will give birth.

Interpretation	You'll pay very dearly if you insist on attempting to do something completely out of your ambit.
Exercise: Reader's Interpretation	
205. Krio Parebul	**mared nɔ go de dans kan mit yu na os, yu go luk am na winda.**
Literal Translation	Marriage will not be dancing, coming to meet you at home, you go looking at it through the window.
Interpretation	Instead of grabbing at a good opportunity, you spend time analyzing it.
Exercise: Reader's Interpretation	
206. Krio Parebul	**mared udat fiba yu mami.**
Literal Translation	Get married to someone who is like your mother.
Interpretation	Self explanatory advice; the idea being that there will be fewer areas of dissent because you are so used to your mother's way of doing things.
Exercise: Reader's Interpretation	

207. Krio Parebul	masta plaba day na os bizabɔdi day na trit.
Literal Translation	Master palaver dies at home, busybody dies in the street.
Interpretation	The one who is directly affected in a matter handles it with discretion, while the sympathiser does not, and ends up with a negative result/ends up in an unenviable position.
Exercise: Reader's Interpretation	
208. Krio Parebul	mɛsenja nɔ ba day na wa.
Literal Translation	A messenger does not die in the war.
Interpretation	I'm only a messenger, so I cannot suffer any ill consequencies because of the contents of the message I bring.
Exercise: Reader's Interpretation	
209. Krio Parebul	mi kak go waka fri, na yu go kɔba yu ɛn.
Literal Translation	My cock will walk freely. It is you who will cover your hen.
Interpretation	Males are free to do whatever they like in relationships. The onus for protection lies with those who are responsible for the females.
Exercise: Reader's Interpretation	

210. Krio Parebul	mi na akpata, yu fɔdɔm pan mi yu go wund; a fɔdɔm pan yu, yu go wund.
Literal Translation	I am a big riverside stone; you fall on me, you'll be wounded; I fall on you, you'll be wounded.
Interpretation	Whatever you do, you can't win. I'll always have the upper hand.
Exercise: Reader's Interpretation	
211. Krio Parebul	miliju farinya lɛk gud sɔl pok.
Literal Translation	Mildewed farinya likes good salted pork. (farinya – food made from roasting grated cassava.)
Interpretation	Referring to a person who wants to enjoy good things which are normally beyond him/her.
Exercise: Reader's Interpretation	
212. Krio Parebul	mis gɔn nɔ de kil. mis bif nɔ de kam na tɔŋ
Literal Translation	A missed gun does not kill. A missed beef (animal) does not come into town.
Interpretation	No result can be achieved if no action is executed.
Exercise: Reader's Interpretation	

213. Krio Parebul	motoka nɔ de big fɔ in drayva. (luk–ɔkrɔ nɔ de langa....)
Literal Translation	A motor car never gets too big for its driver.
Interpretation	One never stops being in a 'subordinate' role in terms of respect, and, to a certain extent, obedience, to one's parents.
Exercise: Reader's Interpretation	
214. Krio Parebul	Mɔmɔ Klɛva ɛn Abu Savis nɔ de slip na nɛt.
Literal Translation	Momoh Clever and Abu Cunning do not sleep at night.
Interpretation	A warning that tricksters do not sleep well because they have to be always on the alert in case their misdeeds are about to catch up with them. Also possibly because they are always planning other shady activities.
Exercise: Reader's Interpretation	
215. Krio Parebul	mɔni na an, bak na grɔn.
Literal Translation	Money in the hand, the back on the ground.
Interpretation	Payment in full before receiving goods or service required.

Exercise: Reader's Interpretation	
216. Krio Parebul	**mɔnki bay pati, pijin bay pia.**
Literal Translation	Monkeys by parties, pigeons by pairs.
Interpretation	People with similar tastes or interests usually like to be together.
Exercise: Reader's Interpretation	
217. Krio Parebul	**mɔnki nɔ ba lɛf in blak an.**
Literal Translation	A monkey does not leave its black hand.
Interpretation	One cannot act against one's nature.
Exercise: Reader's Interpretation	
218. Krio Parebul	**mɔnki nɔ de tɛl in pikin se, 'ol tayt,' we dɛn de ɔp tik, i de tɛl am se, 'luk dɔŋ'.**
Literal Translation	A monkey does not tell its child, 'hold tight', when they are up a tree, it tells it, 'look down'.
Interpretation	Teaching by practical illustration is much more effective than just instructing.
Exercise: Reader's Interpretation	
219. Krio Parebul	**mɔnki tɔk, mɔnki yɛri.**
Literal Translation	A monkey talks, a monkey hears.
Interpretation	Like understands like.

Exercise: Reader's Interpretation	
220. Krio Parebul	**mɔnki trɔsis tayt sote, i mɔs lɛf ples fɔ in tel. (luk– os tayt sote....)**
Literal Translation	No matter how tight a monkey's pair of trousers is, it must (will definitely) leave space for its tail.
Interpretation	There is always a way out if one tries hard enough. There are ways and means!
Exercise: Reader's Interpretation	
221. Krio Parebul	**mɔnki wok babu it.**
Literal Translation	The monkey works, the baboon eats.
Interpretation	Someone reaps the benefits from another person's efforts.
Exercise: Reader's Interpretation	
222. Krio Parebul	**na an de was an bifo an klin.**
Literal Translation	It is hand which washes hand before hand becomes clean.
Interpretation	People need people.
Exercise: Reader's Interpretation	

223. Krio Parebul	na aw dɛn luk yu dɛn go kɔl yu fɔ go tɔn fufu na awujɔ. (bay aw yu drɛs fɔ go awujɔ, na so dɛn go gi yu pɔt fɔ was.)
Literal Translation	It is how they look you, they will call you to go and turn fufu at a ceremonial feast.
Interpretation	How you dress and comport yourself determines how you are treated. Appearances are important.
Exercise: Reader's Interpretation	
224. Krio Parebul	na bɛlful mek pɛtɛtɛ gɛ kanda.
Literal Translation	It is a full belly which makes a potato have a skin.(peel)
Interpretation	You only notice unimportant details when you have everything. Being choosy when you are comfortable.
Exercise: Reader's Interpretation	
225. Krio Parebul	na biɛn kɔnk bak dɛn de gren aligeta pɛpɛ.
Literal Translation	It is behind a snail's back that they grind alligator pepper
Interpretation	Malicious gossip is done in well hidden places.

Exercise: Reader's Interpretation	
226. Krio Parebul	**na bikɔs babu biliv in baksay mek i de swɛla kɔntik. (luk– da dɔg we swɛla...)**
Literal Translation	It is because the baboon believes its backside, that is why it swallows corn stick. (corn on the cob)
Interpretation	One who takes on a big challenge is confident of his/her capability of coping.
Exercise: Reader's Interpretation	
227. Krio Parebul	**na dɛbul drɔma; yu bit am, yu mami day. yu nɔ bit am, yu dadi day. (luk– mi na akpata....)**
Literal Translation	He is a devil drummer; you beat it, your mother dies. You don't beat it, your father dies.
Interpretation	You can't win. Heads you lose. Tails you lose. Whatever happens, you're the loser.
Exercise: Reader's Interpretation	
228. Krio Parebul	**na fut pɔsin kin bɔk, nɔto mɔt.**
Literal Translation	It is the foot a person stubs, not the mouth.

Interpretation	Do not mistakenly divulge secrets which will bring discord.
Exercise: Reader's Interpretation	
229. Krio Parebul	**na krabit man de brok kola na in pɔkit.**
Literal Translation	It is a stingy man who breaks colanut in his pocket.
Interpretation	A mean person keeps his business under cover so that others won't see what he has and beg him.
Exercise: Reader's Interpretation	
230. Krio Parebul	**na libwɛl kil nani got. (luk– na we krikit bɛlful....)**
Literal Translation	It's living well that killed nanny goat.
Interpretation	Living a carefree irresponsible life can have disasterous results.
Exercise: Reader's Interpretation	
231. Krio Parebul	**na lɔv mek tɛn pɔsin it fadin akara.**
Literal Translation	It is love which made tɛn pipul eat one farthing worth of akara. (akara–fried bean cake)

Interpretation	people are generous, longsuffering and forebearing because of love.
Exercise: Reader's Interpretation	
232. Krio Parebul	**na naw yu no se pɔnkin na sup.**
Literal Translation	It is now you know that the pumpkin is soup.
Interpretation	The seemingly unimportant is suddenly appreciated./The value of someone who has been underrated, is realized.
Exercise: Reader's Interpretation	
233. Krio Parebul	**na ren mek got ɛn ship mit na wan ɔndasela. (luk – got ɛn ship nɔ de...)**
Literal Translation	It is rain which made goat and sheep meet in the same cellar.
Interpretation	It is only very unfortunate circumstances which caused people of such different social levels to have any interaction with each other.
Exercise: Reader's Interpretation	
234. Krio Parebul	**na sik lɛk romatizin na in mek dɔg wɛr trɔsis go aks lɛpɛt fɔ dɛt. (na we lɛpɛt gɛ romatizin nain mek ekuru dɔg wɛr solɛ go kɔl dɛt) (luk–we lɛpɛt tit de at nain got kin go kɔl dɛt).**

81

Literal Translation	It is illness like rheumatism which made the dog wear a pair of trousers and went to ask the leopard to pay a debt.
Interpretation	A weak person can approach a strong one when the latter is not in a position to harm him.
Exercise: Reader's Interpretation	
235. Krio Parebul	**na tin kin mek tin bi.**
Literal Translation	It is something which makes something happen.
Interpretation	Remark made when something unusual or outstanding occurs. There is no effect without a cause.
Exercise: Reader's Interpretation	
236. Krio Parebul	**na trɔbul mek babu wes de shayn.**
Literal Translation	It is trouble which caused the baboon's bottom to be shiny.
Interpretation	That person's appearance or condition is the result of hardship. Something happened to cause that person or those people to be in that unenviable state.
Exercise: Reader's Interpretation	

237. Krio Parebul	na trɔbul mek mɔnki cham pɛpɛ.
Literal Translation	It is trouble which made the monkey chew pepper.
Interpretation	Desperate conditions enlicit desperate behaviour.
Exercise: Reader's Interpretation	
238. Krio Parebul	**na wan tin fɔ du akpani, ayda fɔ bwɛl am, ɔ fɔ ros am.**
Literal Translation	There is only one thing to do with akpani. Either it is boiled, or it is roasted.
Interpretation	You do not have much choice in this matter, so there's not much point in wasting time thinking about what to do.
Exercise: Reader's Interpretation	
239. Krio Parebul	**na we kaw nɔ no in trenk, na dat mek i lɛf lili pikin fɔ kɛr am go na fil.**
Literal Translation	It is because the cow does not know its strength, that is why it allowed a little child to take it to a field.
Interpretation	Allowing oneself to be manipulated because the extent of one's authority is not fully realised.

Exercise: Reader's Interpretation	
240. Krio Parebul	**na we krikit bɛlful mek i tek in pɔ bɔs in bɛlɛ. (luk– na libwɛl kil….)**
Literal Translation	It is because the cricket's belly is full, that is why it took its paw to burst its belly.
Interpretation	Living a carefree irresponsible life can be self-desructive.
Exercise: Reader's Interpretation	
241. Krio Parebul	**na we ɔyl ɔt yu go no se akara gɛt ɔmbak.**
Literal Translation	It is when oil is hot, you'll know that akara has a humped back.
Interpretation	People perform optimally in ideal conditions.
Exercise: Reader's Interpretation	
242. Krio Parebul	**na we yu luk yawo in yay, nain yu go si se i de kray. (udat de luk yawo yay, na in no se i de kray.)**
Literal Translation	It is when you look at the bride's eye, that is when you will see that she is crying.
Interpretation	You will only have to feign sympathy When you go out of your way to find out what happened.

Exercise: Reader's Interpretation	
243. Krio Parebul	**na yay de luk wok big.**
Literal Translation	It is the eye which sees that the work is big.
Interpretation	It looks as if it is a lot of work, but once you start, you realize it isn't.
Exercise: Reader's Interpretation	
244. Krio Parebul	**na yay de si yay de sɔri fɔ (r) am.**
Literal Translation	It is the eye which sees the eye, which is sorry for it.
Interpretation	It is people who have to sympathise with the state of other people..
Exercise: Reader's Interpretation	
245. Krio Parebul	**nɛk we nɔ brok go wɛr kɔrin.**
Literal Translation	A neck which is not broken will wear decorative shells and beads.
Interpretation	As long as one has one's health and strength, one has a chance to make things work; a fighting chance to succeed in life. While theres' life there's hope.
Exercise: Reader's Interpretation	

246. Krio Parebul	nɛt san nɔ de dray klos.
Literal Translation	Night sun does not dry clothes.
Interpretation	Something which is non-existent will not produce the desired effect. Wishful thinking.
Exercise: Reader's Interpretation	
247. Krio Parebul	no yusɛf nɔto kɔs, na gud advays.
Literal Translation	Know yourself is not an abuse, it is good advice.
Interpretation	It is good to be fully aware of one's abilities and capability. /be mindful of where one is seen, and with whom one associates.
Exercise: Reader's Interpretation	
248. Krio Parebul	nɔ abop pan dayman sus.
Literal Translation	Do not have hopes on a dead man's shoe.
Interpretation	Do not put your hopes on something you can't be sure of.
Exercise: Reader's Interpretation	
249. Krio Parebul	nɔ aks mareduman u gi am bɛlɛ.
Literal Translation	Do not ask a married woman who made her pregnant.
Interpretation	Don't ask the obvious.

Exercise: Reader's Interpretation	
250. Krio Parebul	**nɔ bring gladi na bɛrin os.**
Literal Translation	Do not bring happiness to a house of mourning.
Interpretation	Do not act with levity or make facetious remarks when extremely distressing matters are being discussed.
Exercise: Reader's Interpretation	
251. Krio Parebul	**nɔ de luk ɔp klawd fɔ sɔntin we yu go fɛn na grɔn.**
Literal Translation	Don't keep looking up in the clouds for something you can find on the ground.
Interpretation	Don't overlook the obvious.
Exercise: Reader's Interpretation	
252. Krio Parebul	**nɔ ɛng yu kotoku na say we yu an nɔ de rich. (nɔ put tin usay yu an nɔ de rich)**
Literal Translation	Do not hang your money bag where your hand cannot reach.
Interpretation	Don't try to live beyond your means. Cut your coat according to your cloth.
Exercise: Reader's Interpretation	

253. Krio Parebul	nɔ kray pas udat gɛ bɛrin.
Literal Translation	Do not cry more than the ones who are bereaved.
Interpretation	Do not act as if what is happening affects you more than the people whose business it is.
Exercise: Reader's Interpretation	
254. Krio Parebul	nɔ mek kata we lod nɔ de. (luk– yu de prɛd mata....)
Literal Translation	Do not make a headring on which to put loads, when there isn't a load.
Interpretation	Do not treat as certainty something which might never happen.
Exercise: Reader's Interpretation	
255. Krio Parebul	nɔ pul bred na mi mɔt we yu nɔ gɛt biskit fɔ put de.
Literal Translation	Do not pull bread out of my mouth when you do not have a biscuit to put there.
Interpretation	Do not lure me out of a situation unless you have something better in store for me.
Exercise: Reader's Interpretation	

256. Krio Parebul	nɔ pul shɔt we fɛt nɔ mit yu.
Literal Translation	Don't take off your shirt when a fight has not met you(there is not yet a fight)
Interpretation	Do not take action in anticipation of an unpleasant event which might not even occur.
Exercise: Reader's Interpretation	
257. Krio Parebul	nɔto bikɔs mi mami sik mek a go lik dɔkta wes.
Literal Translation	It is not because my mother is sick that I will lick a doctor's bottom.
Interpretation	I am not so desperate that I will do such a demeaning act.
Exercise: Reader's Interpretation	
258. Krio Parebul	nɔto mi mɔt yu go kan yɛri se nyu yams bɔs na fam.
Literal Translation	It is not from my mouth you will come and hear that new yams have sprouted in the farm.
Interpretation	I refuse to make any comment on that piece of news/gossip.
Exercise: Reader's Interpretation	
259. Krio Parebul	nyanga gɛt pen.
Literal Translation	Making oneself beautiful is painful.

Interpretation	To look nice, you often have to suffer some inconvenience, discomfort or even pain.
Exercise: Reader's Interpretation	
260. Krio Parebul	**nyu brum swip klin; ol brum no ɔi di kɔna.**
Literal Translation	A new broom sweeps clean; an old broom knows all the corners.
Interpretation	A new person has refreshingly new ideas, but the previous person knows all the inner workings, contacts, and how to push the right buttons to get things done.
Exercise: Reader's Interpretation	
261. Krio Parebul	**nyu lɔv nɔ no bɛn wes.**
Literal Translation	A new love does not know (notice) bent hips.
Interpretation	Love is blind.
Exercise: Reader's Interpretation	
262. Krio Parebul	**ogiri de kɔs kenda se i smɛl.**
Literal Translation	Ogiri is abusing kenda that it smells. (ogiri-ground and fermented beni-seed. Kenda- African locust bean. Both used in cooking

Interpretation	Pot calling the kettle black.
Exercise: Reader's Interpretation	
263. Krio Parebul	**ol dɔg nɔ de lan nyu nem.**
Literal Translation	An old dog does not learn a new name.
Interpretation	It is well-nigh impossible to get people who are old and set in their ways, to acquire new habits.
Exercise: Reader's Interpretation	
264. Krio Parebul	**ol fayawud nɔ ba at fɔ kech.**
Literal Translation	Old (i.e-used) firewood is not hard to catch (fire).
Interpretation	It is very easy to revive a previous amorous relationship.
Exercise: Reader's Interpretation	
265. Krio Parebul	**ol mami sidɔm te, i de si fa pas pikin we klem tik. (luk– pikin tinap....)**
Literal Translation	An old woman sitting down can see further than a child who has climbed a tree.
Interpretation	Older people are much wiser than youth, by virtue of their age and experience.
Exercise: Reader's Interpretation	

266. Krio Parebul	oluman wan day yu go tek tik wap am. (luk– bɔd wan flay yu go shek tik) (got kaka wan rol yu go kik am.)
Literal Translation	An old woman is near to death, you go and take a stick and hit her hard.
Interpretation	Something is about to happen and you precipitate the event by your action.
Exercise: Reader's Interpretation	
267. Krio Parebul	os tayt sote fɔl go le.
Literal Translation	No matter how tight a house, the fowl will lay.
Interpretation	No matter how difficult the situation, one can always find a way to get round it. There are ways and means.
Exercise: Reader's Interpretation	
268. Krio Parebul	ɔg de aks in mami wetin mek in mɔt lɔŋ. i se wet, yu go si am fɔ yusɛf.
Literal Translation	The hog is asking its mother why her mouth is long. She says, 'wait, you will see it for yourself.'
Interpretation	Response to child asking about heredity traits; meaning, you'll know as you get older, because the same thing will happen to you.
Exercise: Reader's Interpretation	

269. Krio Parebul	ɔkrɔ nɔ de langa pas in masta.
Literal Translation	Okra is never longer than its master.
Interpretation	No matter how old, one is always, to some extent, in a position of subordination to one's parents.
Exercise: Reader's Interpretation	
270. Krio Parebul	ɔl dɛn flawa pɔt we de na banana wes bin de na shoglas.
Literal Translation	All those flower pots which are at the foot of the banana tree, were once in a shop's window display.
Interpretation	We all have our day of glory, and then get old and are not as useful. Being at one's peak does not last forever.
Exercise: Reader's Interpretation	
271. Krio Parebul	ɔl kabɔ na kabɔ. (luk– ɔl kray du....)
Literal Translation	All greetings are greetings.
Interpretation	One thing will do just as well as another of the same kind.
Exercise: Reader's Interpretation	
272. Krio Parebul	ɔl kaw blak na nɛt.
Literal Translation	All cows are black at night.

Interpretation	It is not easy to distinguish one thing from another at night. People who all seem to behave the same way in a particular environment, may be seen to behave differently when the situation changes./also, one can misinterpret.
Exercise: Reader's Interpretation	
273. Krio Parebul	**ɔl kondo le in bɛlɛ na grɔn, yu nɔ no uswan in yon de at am.**
Literal Translation	All lizards lay their belly on the ground, you do not know which one's belly is hurting it.
Interpretation	You can't tell which people have problems just by looking at them.
Exercise: Reader's Interpretation	
274. Krio Parebul	**ɔl kray du fɔ bɛrin. (luk– ɔl kabɔ na ....)**
Literal Translation	All crying will do for a bereavement.
Interpretation	One thing will do just as well as another of the same kind.
Exercise: Reader's Interpretation	
275. Krio Parebul	**ɔl rare na rare. (rare nɔ pas rare)**
Literal Translation	All prostitution is prostitution.
Interpretation	What I am doing is no worse than what you are doing.

Exercise: Reader's Interpretation	
276. Krio Parebul	**ɔlman fɔ insɛf Gɔd fɔ wi ɔl.**
Literal Translation	Everybody for himself, God for us all.
Interpretation	Some people will only seek their own interests.
Exercise: Reader's Interpretation	
277. Krio Parebul	**ɔltɛm fɔ tifman, wan de fɔ masta os.**
Literal Translation	All the time for a thief, one day for the master of the house.
Interpretation	Wrong doers will definitely get caught sooner or later.
Exercise: Reader's Interpretation	
278. Krio Parebul	**ɔri ɔri bɔs trɔsis.**
Literal Translation	Hurry, hurry, bursts trousers.
Interpretation	Advising that being in too much of a hurry might cause accidents. Much haste less speed.
Exercise: Reader's Interpretation	
279. Krio Parebul	**ɔrinch nɔ de bia lɛm.**
Literal Translation	Orange (tree) does not bear lime (fruit).
Interpretation	Like father like son. Chip of the old block.

Exercise: Reader's Interpretation	
280. Krio Parebul	**pamayn go na wayt plet nain i bigin prεd. (pamayn nɔ bin no se i go go na wayt plet).**
Literal Translation	Palmoil goes on a white plate, and it begins to spread. (Palmoil didn't know that it would go on a white plate.)
Interpretation	Said of someone catapaulted into an elevated position, who then starts showing off and overstepping boundaries.
Exercise: Reader's Interpretation	
281. Krio Parebul	**pasmak sɔl nɔ de mek sup swit.**
Literal Translation	Too much salt does not make the soup sweet.(soup=any sauce or gravy)
Interpretation	Advocating moderation in everything.
Exercise: Reader's Interpretation	
282. Krio Parebul	**peshεnt dɔg it fat bon.**
Literal Translation	The patient dog eats a fat bone. (The patient dog is the one who will eat........)
Interpretation	Exercising patience brings just rewards. Good things come to those who wait.

Exercise: Reader's Interpretation	
283. Krio Parebul	**pikin tinap i nɔ si natin; bigman butu i si fawe. (bigman we sidɔm de si pas pikin we tinap) (luk-ol mami sidɔm ....)**
Literal Translation	A child standing up does not see anything; a crouching adult sees far.
Interpretation	Adults are much wiser than youth, by virtue of their age and experience in life.
Exercise: Reader's Interpretation	
284. Krio Parebul	**pikin we nɔ de de na os, dɛn go sho am in mami grev.**
Literal Translation	A child who is never at home, They will show him/her his/her mother's grave.
Interpretation	A child who is never at home, will realize, too late, that there is no opportunity of reclaiming what has been lost./ one who is consistently not present where one's presence is necessary, ends up in a situation where there is no opportunity of reclaiming what has been lost.
Exercise: Reader's Interpretation	

285. Krio Parebul	pikin we nɔ de yɛri in mami wɔd, na trit go mɛn am.(pikin we nɔ de yɛri wɔd na os, na trit go tren am).
Literal Translation	A child who does not listen to its mother's words, it is the street which will bring it up.
Interpretation	A child who does not listen and try to obey what is taught at home, will get hard knocks from the world.
Exercise: Reader's Interpretation	
286. Krio Parebul	pikin we sabi was in an go it wit bigman.
Literal Translation	A child who knows how to wash his/her hands will eat with important people.
Interpretation	Children who know how to behave and play their cards right, will mingle with influential people.
Exercise: Reader's Interpretation	
287. Krio Parebul	pikin we se in mami nɔ go slip, insɛf nɔ go slip.
Literal Translation	A child who says his/her mother will not sleep, he himself/herself will not sleep.

Interpretation	If you create a stressful situation, you are definitely part of it, and will yourself suffer any ill effects.
Exercise: Reader's Interpretation	
288. Krio Parebul	**pikin we wan wɛr in dadi trɔsis, na rop go it in wes. (da pikin we wan wɛr bigman trɔsis.....) (luk–da kak we wan kro........)**
Literal Translation	A child who wants to wear its father's trousers, it is rope which will eat into its waist.
Interpretation	A child who wants to do something before he is old enough to do it, will suffer adverse consequences./ will find him/herself in serious trouble.
Exercise: Reader's Interpretation	
289. Krio Parebul	**pikɔk sho fayn fɛda, gini–ɛn pre fɔ lɔŋ layf. (luk– tolotolo pre fɔ ....)**
Literal Translation	The peacock shows fine feathers, the guinea hen prays for long life.
Interpretation	Having different priorities.
Exercise: Reader's Interpretation	
290. Krio Parebul	**pit am na bif; swɛla am na bon.**
Literal Translation	Spit it, it is beef; swallow it, it is bone.

Interpretation	Not appreciating what one has until it is lost.
Exercise: Reader's Interpretation	
291. Krio Parebul	**pit wet pit, swɛla blɔd.**
Literal Translation	Spit white spit, swallow blood.
Interpretation	Show the world a sunny face, hide your pain. Don't express your deepest feelings.
Exercise: Reader's Interpretation	
292. Krio Parebul	**ple ple kil bɔd; day bɔd kuk sup.**
Literal Translation	Play play kills bird, dead bird is cooked in soup.
Interpretation	something done as a joke, can have tragic results.
Exercise: Reader's Interpretation	
293. Krio Parebul	**poman gɛt ɔged. i ɛng am na fɛnch.**
Literal Translation	A poor man has a hog's head. He hangs it on a fence. (i.e for all to see)
Interpretation	When a poor person has good fortune, he wants everyone to know how far he's come up in the world.
Exercise: Reader's Interpretation	

294. Krio Parebul	pɔnkin nɔ gɛ natin fɔ ayd pan nɛf. (luk–wetin de pan yams...)
Literal Translation	Pumpkin does not have anything to hide from knife.
Interpretation	There are no secrets here. This party knows absolutely everything about the other.
Exercise: Reader's Interpretation	
295. Krio Parebul	pɔsin nɔ go tot yu na bak yu se in ed de smɛl.
Literal Translation	A person will not be carrying you on his back, you say his head is smelling.
Interpretation	You can't say negative things about someone who is helping you in a big way. Ungratefulness.
Exercise: Reader's Interpretation	
296. Krio Parebul	push yanda bɛtɛ pas ɛmti bed. (shub yanda...) (luk–bad man bɛtɛ pas ɛmti os)
Literal Translation	'Push away from me', is better than an empty bed.
Interpretation	It is preferable to have a man around, even if you are quarrelling, than have no one at all.
Exercise: Reader's Interpretation	

297. Krio Parebul	put yams na faya tek yay de fɛn nɛf.
Literal Translation	Put yams on the fire, take eyes to find the knife.
Interpretation	Don't wait until everything is in place before you start doing what you want to do. Start with whatever you have, while trying to see how you can get everything else done.
Exercise: Reader's Interpretation	
298. Krio Parebul	put yu yay dɔŋ mek yu si yu nos.
Literal Translation	Put your eyes down so that you can see your nose.
Interpretation	You have to make strenuous effort to achieve anything worthwhile. You will not succeed if you do not stop fooling around.
Exercise: Reader's Interpretation	
299. Krio Parebul	ren nɔ de fɔdɔm na wan man domɔt.
Literal Translation	Rain does not fall down on (only) one man's door.
Interpretation	No one person has a monopoly on misfortune
Exercise: Reader's Interpretation	
300. Krio Parebul	rɛspɛkt pas bɛlful.
Literal Translation	Respect is better than a full belly.

Interpretation	Commanding respect is better than having a wealth of material goods.
Exercise: Reader's Interpretation	
301. Krio Parebul	**rod lɔŋ sote i mɔs bɛn.**
Literal Translation	No matter how long a road is, it will have a bend.
Interpretation	Nothing lasts forever.
Exercise: Reader's Interpretation	
302. Krio Parebul	**rop nɔ fit fɔl nɛk, nain mek dɛn tay am na in fut.**
Literal Translation	A rope does not fit the fowl's neck, that is why they tie it on its foot.
Interpretation	This responsibility/ trouble is not meant for such as you.
Exercise: Reader's Interpretation	
303. Krio Parebul	**rɔb mi bak a rɔb yu yon. (luk– fɔdɔm fɔ mi a fɔdɔm fɔ yu.)**
Literal Translation	Rob my back, I rob your own.
Interpretation	Seek my interests and I'll seek yours.
Exercise: Reader's Interpretation	
304. Krio Parebul	**rɔtinbɔdi blant Jizɔs.**
Literal Translation	A rottening body belongs to Jesus.

Interpretation	I didn't get a look in when things were going well, but now when this person is in this unenviable state, it is I who am expected to take over./Only Jesus will gladly cope with someone in such an appalling state.
Exercise: Reader's Interpretation	
305. Krio Parebul	**sabi nɔ gɛ wɔri. – na bikful gɛ waala.**
Literal Translation	To know has no worries. It is being a fool that has problems.
Interpretation	When you know how to do something, you don't have problems. It's only when you don't know, that you're in trouble. Only the fool has problems.
Exercise: Reader's Interpretation	
306. Krio Parebul	**saful saful kech mɔnki.**
Literal Translation	Gently, gently, catch the monkey.
Interpretation	One is much more likely to achieve desired results by being very very careful.
Exercise: Reader's Interpretation	
307. Krio Parebul	**ship ed ɛn got ed nɔto wan.**
Literal Translation	A sheep's head and a goat's head are not the same.

Interpretation	What happens to one person can be quite different from what happens to another person in the same situation. Their 'luck' is different./ what is good for one person might not be good for another.
Exercise: Reader's Interpretation	
308. Krio Parebul	**shɔtat man nɔ de jɔyn kakadɛbul. (luk-if yu nɔ want mɔnki tel.....)**
Literal Translation	A short tempered man does not enrol at a Kakadevil society .
Interpretation	Don't associate yourself with what you deem might be be undesirable company, if you know you are short-tempered.
Exercise: Reader's Interpretation	
309. Krio Parebul	**shrawd nɔ gɛ pɔkit. (kɔfin nɔ gɛ kɔbɔd)**
Literal Translation	A shroud does not have pockets.
Interpretation	You cannot take anything away with you when you die, so all this grabbing for material goods, in the end does not mean anything.
Exercise: Reader's Interpretation	

310. Krio Parebul	sidɔn luk nɔ de rɔtin wes.
Literal Translation	Sitting down looking does not rot the bottom.
Interpretation	No harm comes by just observing, but a lot of good can be learnt.
Exercise: Reader's Interpretation	
311. Krio Parebul	sɔl nɔ de prez insɛf na sup.
Literal Translation	Salt does not praise itself when it is in a soup.
Interpretation	You do not need to extol your good works. Results speak for themselves.
Exercise: Reader's Interpretation	
312. Krio Parebul	sɔri–at bombo bɔn basta pikin.
Literal Translation	A kind–hearted vagina will give birth to a bastard child.
Interpretation	It does not pay to be too compassionate, as that might produce unwanted results. Also, frivolous sex has very serious undesirable consequencies.
Exercise: Reader's Interpretation	
313. Krio Parebul	sup swit na mɔni kil am
Literal Translation	Soup which is very sweet, it is money which kills it.

Interpretation	A dish is very tasty because a lot of money has been spent on it./ A fair amount of money is needed to produce anything which is exceptionally good.
Exercise: Reader's Interpretation	
314. Krio Parebul	**tap fɔ dans we dɛn stil de bit. (nɔ dans te bata tap fɔ bit)**
Literal Translation	Stop dancing when they are still beating.
Interpretation	Don't wait until you are pushed out or until everyone has had enough of you. Bow out when you are stil being acclaimed.
Exercise: Reader's Interpretation	
315. Krio Parebul	**tek day mɔnki skyad babu. (tek day babu skyad lɛpɛt)**
Literal Translation	Take a dead monkey to scare a baboon.
Interpretation	Trying to use scare tactics which nobody is afraid of.
Exercise: Reader's Interpretation	

316. Krio Parebul	tek tɛm kil anch yu go si in gɔt.
Literal Translation	Very carefully kill an ant, you will see its entrails.
Interpretation	If you are painstakingly meticulous, you will achieve your goal, no matter how impossible it might seem.
Exercise: Reader's Interpretation	

317. Krio Parebul	tide fɔ yu tumara fɔ mi.
Literal Translation	Today for you, tomorrow for me.
Interpretation	Every dog has his day.
Exercise: Reader's Interpretation	

318. Krio Parebul	tif tif Gɔd laf.
Literal Translation	Steal, steal, God laughs.
Interpretation	You steal something, and then someone else steals it from you.
Exercise: Reader's Interpretation	

319. Krio Parebul	tik te na wata sote i nɔ go tɔn aligeta.
Literal Translation	It doesn't matter how long a stick stays in water, it will never change into an alligator.

Interpretation	No matter how much you strive to blend into a new environment, you will never actually become different from what you were born. Also, one's intrinsic characteristics never change. A leopard doesn't change its spots.
Exercise: Reader's Interpretation	
320. Krio Parebul	**tin de bɛn wan we big pas tu, na da sem tin de sɛvin si bɛn siks we mek et twis. (na di trɔbul we siks ɛn sɛvin si, nain mek et twis)**
Literal Translation	There is something behind one which is bigger than two; that is the same thing that seven saw behind siks which made eight to be twisted.
Interpretation	One really cannot get to the bottom of this. This problem is indeed an enigma./ difficult to figure out. Everyone has his/her challenges.
Exercise: Reader's Interpretation	
321. Krio Parebul	**tit ɛn tɔŋ mɔs jam.**
Literal Translation	Teeth and tongue must (will definitely) come into collision.

Interpretation	There are bound to be disagreements in all close relationships. The very nature of close relationships necessitates fallings out.
Exercise: Reader's Interpretation	
322. Krio Parebul	**tit mek bifo trɔbul. (luk– tit nɔ de munin)**
Literal Translation	Teeth were made before trouble.
Interpretation	Even in the midst of trouble, there are always lighthearted interludes.
Exercise: Reader's Interpretation	
323. Krio Parebul	**tit nɔ de munin. (luk– tit mek bifo trɔbul)**
Literal Translation	Teeth do not mourn.
Interpretation	No matter how somber the atmosphere, there is always a window of mirth.
Exercise: Reader's Interpretation	
324. Krio Parebul	**Tolotolo pre fɔ fayn fɛda, gini fɔl pre fɔ lɔŋ layf. (luk– pikɔk sho fayn.....)**
Literal Translation	The turkey prays for fine feathers, the guinea fowl prays for long life.

Interpretation	Having different priorities.
Exercise: Reader's Interpretation	
325. Krio Parebul	**totonja man wɔd nɔ ba pas na frɔkot man kɔntri.**
Literal Translation	A man who wears a loincloth does not have much say in the country of the man who wears a suit.
Interpretation	A poor/junior man's words are never acceptable to his superiors.
Exercise: Reader's Interpretation	
326. Krio Parebul	**tɔk na osusu.**
Literal Translation	Talk is osusu. (osusu—money put into a private fund at regular intervals by several individuals, and the accumulated amount withdrawn in turns.
Interpretation	Be careful how you talk, especially when another person suffers calamity. It might be your turn one day. You get back what you put in; as you express your ideas, you should be equally prepared to receive other peoples.
Exercise: Reader's Interpretation	

327. Krio Parebul	tranga sik want tranga mɛrɛsin. (luk-bad mɛrɛsin na in fɔ tek mɛn bad sofut.)
Literal Translation	Strong illness wants strong medicine.
Interpretation	Harsh solutions are needed to solve difficult problems.
Exercise: Reader's Interpretation	

328. Krio Parebul	tray fɔ yu ed mek yu fut go kɔba.
Literal Translation	Try for your head so that your foot will be covered.
Interpretation	Always aim high to ensure you have enough to cover all your needs./ do not depend on another person's success or more favourable situation.
Exercise: Reader's Interpretation	

329. Krio Parebul	trik na smok.
Literal Translation	A habit is like smoke.
Interpretation	Habits cannot be hidden for long; they soon appear in the open.
Exercise: Reader's Interpretation	

330. Krio Parebul	trit nɔ gɛ tit bɔt i de bɛt. (luk– ɛni gyal pikin we wan put in yay na trit....)
Literal Translation	The street does not have teeth, but it bites.
Interpretation	The world can teach hard lessons.
Exercise: Reader's Interpretation	
331. Krio Parebul	**trɔbul de slip, nyanga go wek am.**
Literal Translation	Trouble is asleep, nyanga goes and wakes him.
Interpretation	All is well and someone deliberately disturbs the peace / causes disharmony.
Exercise: Reader's Interpretation	
332. Krio Parebul	**trɔbul nɔ mek fɔ tik ɛn ston.**
Literal Translation	Trouble was not made for sticks and stones.
Interpretation	Implied admonishment to be strong when problems come, because as long as we are human beings, they will come.
Exercise: Reader's Interpretation	
333. Krio Parebul	**trɔki wan bɔks bɔt in an shɔt.**
Literal Translation	The tortoise wants to box, but its hand is short.

Interpretation	Not having the means, or be in a position to do what one wants to do.
Exercise: Reader's Interpretation	
334. Krio Parebul	**tu lɔŋnos man nɔ de kis.**
Literal Translation	Two long-nosed men don't kiss.
Interpretation	people with similar character traits will not get on with each other.
Exercise: Reader's Interpretation	
335. Krio Parebul	**tu-yay man nɔ si gɔvna.**
Literal Translation	Two-eyed man does not see the governor. (implied - you have only one eye.)
nterpretation	When a person with limited gifts or means, aims too high, he is reminded that even those who have greater claims have not yet achieved this.
Exercise: Reader's Interpretation	
336. Krio Parebul	**u bɔbɔ go papa, u titi go mama.**
Literal Translation	Who is a boy will be a father; who is a girl will be a mother.

Interpretation	Warning to children that they will grow up and be at the receiving end of what their parents are now experiencing. Especially when children misbehave, or are being too demanding, unhelpful, unco-operative etc.
Exercise: Reader's Interpretation	
337. Krio Parebul	**u bɔn dɔg? na dɔg.**
Literal Translation	Who gave birth to a dog? It is a dog.
Interpretation	Reffering to hereditary traits in a derogatory manner.
Exercise: Reader's Interpretation	
338. Krio Parebul	**u bɔn twin, na in go no aw fɔ gi dɛn bɔbi.**
Literal Translation	The one who gives birth to twins is the one who will know how to give them breasts. (breastfeed them).
Interpretation	The person in a tricky situation is in the best position to handle it.
Exercise: Reader's Interpretation	
339. Krio Parebul	**u gi dɔg ɔn?**
Literal Translation	Who gave the dog horns? (sarcasm)

Interpretation	I cannot possibly set my sights that high; that is way beyond my capabilities./or you, he, she cannot possibly.............
Exercise: Reader's Interpretation	
340. Krio Parebul	**u kɔl yu pan mared we yu tek rɔsti tre fɔ kan sav.**
Literal Translation	Who called (invited) you to the wedding that you take a rusty tray to come and serve.
Interpretation	This has nothing to do with you, and you don't have any part in this business, so kindly keep your distance.
Exercise: Reader's Interpretation	
341. Krio Parebul	**u trowe asis na in asis go fala.**
Literal Translation	The one who throws ashes, is the one whom ashes will follow.
Interpretation	He who injures others will himself be injured at some point of time in the future.
Exercise: Reader's Interpretation	
342. Krio Parebul	**u waka pan pamayn, na in fut go rɛd.**
Literal Translation	The one who walks on palmoil, is the one whose foot will be red.

Interpretation	The person who does the act is the one on whom will be reflected any resulting effects.
Exercise: Reader's Interpretation	
343. Krio Parebul	**uman ampa nɔ ba lɛf biɛn.**
Literal Translation	A woman's hamper is never left behind.
Interpretation	A woman, by virtue of being a woman, can always find someone to take care of her. (Implication – a man.)
Exercise: Reader's Interpretation	
344. Krio Parebul	**uman nɔ ba nem Jɔn fɔ natin.**
Literal Translation	A woman is not called John for nothing.(ie without reason)
Interpretation	Reffering to a woman who dares to undertake what are regarded as a man's responsibility.
Exercise: Reader's Interpretation	
345. Krio Parebul	**usay de pan yams we nɛf nɔ no. (wetin de pan yams we nɛf nɔ no.) (luk– wetin de pan nɛk...)**
Literal Translation	What part of yams does knife not know.

117

Interpretation	Someone claiming to know everything about the person in question – with sexual inuendos.
Exercise: Reader's Interpretation	
346. Krio Parebul	**usay yu bin de we Joki Banda de bɔn?**
Literal Translation	Where were you when Joki Banda was burning?
Interpretation	You weren't around when any of this was happening, so you don't know anything about the matter. This is none of your business!
Exercise: Reader's Interpretation	
347. Krio Parebul	**uswan na mi yon pan ɔg mɔni – we mi dadi nɔto bucha.**
Literal Translation	What is my own with hog's money? (when my father is not a butcher)
Interpretation	That is none of my business. I am not getting involved.
Exercise: Reader's Interpretation	
348. Krio Parebul	**waka fɔ natin bɛtɛ pas sidɔm fɔ natin. (luk– wes nɔ de gi.....)**
Literal Translation	Walking for nothing is better than sitting down for nothing.

Interpretation	You stand a better chance of having something if you are moving around, than if you are sitting down doing nothing.
Exercise: Reader's Interpretation	
349. Krio Parebul	**wan-an banguls nɔ ba shek.**
Literal Translation	A single bracelet does not shake.
Interpretation	It takes at least two, to quarrel.
Exercise: Reader's Interpretation	
350. Krio Parebul	**wan an nɔ de tay bɔndul. (luk- wan finga .....)**
Literal Translation	One hand does not tie a bundle.
Interpretation	You cannot do by yourself, something which demands the co-operation of several people.
Exercise: Reader's Interpretation	
351. Krio Parebul	**wan finga nɔ de kech lɔs. (....nɔ de pik lɔs na ed.) (luk- wan an nɔ de....)**
Literal Translation	One finger does not catch lice.
Interpretation	You cannot do by yourself, something which demands the co-operation of several people.
Exercise: Reader's Interpretation	

352. Krio Parebul	was ɔlsay pan pikin, lɛf in wes fɔ in mami.
Literal Translation	Wash everywhere on a child, but leave its bottom for its mother.
Interpretation	Know where to draw the line concerning someone else's business. Caution not to overpresume on your authority over someone else's child.
Exercise: Reader's Interpretation	
353. Krio Parebul	wata nɔ de dɔti fɔ natin.
Literal Translation	Water does not get dirty for nothing.
Interpretation	Unpalatabe conditions don't exist without cause. / Behind every ugly rumour, there is usually a basis of truth.
Exercise: Reader's Interpretation	
354. Krio Parebul	wata trowe bɔt kalbas nɔ brok.
Literal Translation	The water spilt, but the calabash is not broken.
Interpretation	Said to comfort someone who has had a miscarriage, or some other misfortune. All is not lost.
Exercise: Reader's Interpretation	

355. Krio Parebul	wata wam te, i nɔ go bɔn bambu os.
Literal Translation	No matter how hot the water is, it will not burn a bamboo house.
Interpretation	No matter how good a substance is, it has its limitations, and will be ineffective beyond those limits.
Exercise: Reader's Interpretation	
356. Krio Parebul	wata we na fɔ yu, nɔ go rɔn pas yu.
Literal Translation	Water which is for you, will not run past you.
Interpretation	No matter what happens, you will always get what you are destined to have.
Exercise: Reader's Interpretation	
357. Krio Parebul	watasay ston nɔ de fred ren.
Literal Translation	A stone which is on the banks of a brook or stream, is not afraid of rain.
Interpretation	Being part of an environment, nothing from that environment is strange, so one can therefore easily cope with things of a similar nature.
Exercise: Reader's Interpretation	

358. Krio Parebul	we anch wan alaki, i go pul wing nain bɔd si am fɔ chuk am. (luk– we kakroch wan alaki....)
Literal Translation	When the ant wants to bring trouble on itself, it sprouts wings, then the bird sees it and stabs it .
Interpretation	Some people seek out trouble. Comport themselves in a way which lands them in serious trouble.
359. Krio Parebul	we binch rɔ i nɔ ful blay!
Literal Translation	When beans are raw they don't fill up a baskɛt. (implied– they won't when they are dried)
Interpretation	When conditions were most favourable, you didn't achieve your goal, you won't when they are less favourable.
360. Krio Parebul	we blɛnyay man se i go ston yu, i dɔn mas ston.
Literal Translation	When a blind man says he will stone you he has stepped on a stone.
Interpretation	If someone says he'll do something which seems impossible for him to do, it is because he has very tangible reasons to know that he can do it.

Exercise: Reader's Interpretation	
361. Krio Parebul	**we briz de kɛr mataodo, wetin fana de fɛn na grɔn. (if briz kɛr mataodo, nɔto fana i go lɛf) (luk– we tinada de ker ton os ruf....)**
Literal Translation	When breeze is carrying away the wooden mortar, what is a winnower finding on the ground?
Interpretation	This has caused big trouble for very important or powerful people, how much more will it not affect the weak and defenceless.
Exercise: Reader's Interpretation	
362. Krio Parebul	**we frɔg yɔŋ i nɔ gɛ wes.**
Literal Translation	When the frɔg is young it does not have a nicely rounded bottom. (implied– it won't have one when it is old)
Interpretation	You haven't been doing this, or been able to do this when you were young, so you definitely will be in no position to do it when you are older. what wasn't achieved when you were in your prime, will not be achieved when you are in your decline.

Exercise: Reader's Interpretation	
363. Krio Parebul	**we kakroch wan alaki na insay pamayn bɔtul i kin go. (luk– we anch….)**
Literal Translation	When the cockroach wants to find trouble for itself, it is inside a palmoil bottle it goes.
Interpretation	Said of one whose deliberate action gets him/herslf into serious trouble.
Exercise: Reader's Interpretation	
364. Krio Parebul	**we lɛpɛt tit de at am, nain got kin go kɔl dɛt. (luk– na sik lɛk romatizin…)**
Literal Translation	When the leopard's teeth is hurting it, that is when goat goes to ask for payment of debt.
Interpretation	A weak person can approach a strong one when the latter is not in a position to harm him.
Exercise: Reader's Interpretation	
365. Krio Parebul	**we pus nɔ de arata tek chaj.**
Literal Translation	When puss is not there, rat puts himself in charge.
Interpretation	When the boss/leader is not there, an underling takes over and starts calling the shots.

Exercise: Reader's Interpretation	
366. Krio Parebul	**we tinada de kɛr ton os ruf, nɔto fɔl tel i nɔ go bɛn. (luk– we briz....)**
Literal Translation	When a tornado is taking off the roof of a stone house, it is not the tail of a fowl that it will not bend.
Interpretation	When some misfortune hits the strong and powerful, how much more will it not affect the weak and defenceless.
Exercise: Reader's Interpretation	
367. Krio Parebul	**we wata nɔ gɛda na yay, aw i go fɔdɔm na chɛst? (we wata nɔ sɛt na yay, i nɔ go drɔp na jɔ.)**
Literal Translation	When water does not gather in the eye, how will it drop on the chest?
Interpretation	Said of persons who pretend to be affected by an experience when they really are not. Also, one cannot give what one doesn't have.
Exercise: Reader's Interpretation	
368. Krio Parebul	**we yu fɔdɔm na wata, na fɔ was.**
Literal Translation	When you fall into water, you should wash.

Interpretation	Make the best of an unfortunate situation in which you inadvertently find yourself. Use your predicament to your advantage.
Exercise: Reader's Interpretation	
369. Krio Parebul	**we yu nɔ gɛt dɔg fɔ go ɔntin, yu go tek got.**
Literal Translation	When you do not have a dog to take hunting, you will take a goat.
Interpretation	If the usual route is not available, try something else. Be innovative.
Exercise: Reader's Interpretation	
370. Krio Parebul	**we yu si ɔkpɔlɔ klem tik, mɔs no se grɔn wam. (we yu si ɔkpɔlɔ jomp fɛnch.....)**
Literal Translation	When you see a frog climbing a tree, know that the ground is warm/hot.
Interpretation	People will do unusual things/ act out of character, to get out of difficulty or escape danger. If a person does something unusual, there must be a good reason for doing it.
Exercise: Reader's Interpretation	

371. Krio Parebul	we yu si trɔbul sidɔm na amɔk, nɔ ledɔm nia (r) am.
Literal Translation	When you see trouble sitting in a hammock, don't lie down near it.
Interpretation	Don't go looking for trouble. Don't stir up a hornet's nest.
Exercise: Reader's Interpretation	
372. Krio Parebul	we yu si yu kɔmpin os de kech faya, na fɔ ib wata.
Literal Translation	When you see your companion's house burning, you should throw water.
Interpretation	Be interested in what is happening around you, especially in times of distress. Empathise with others.
Exercise: Reader's Interpretation	
373. Krio Parebul	we yu wan kɔs dɛfyes man, kɔs am na in pikin yes.
Literal Translation	When you want to abuse a deaf man, do it in the hearing of his child.
Interpretation	If you think you might have difficulty getting through to someone to deliver some unpleasant home truths, have your say in the presence of the person's close associates, and what you say will definitely get to its target.

Exercise: Reader's Interpretation	
374. Krio Parebul	**wes nɔ de gi na fut de gi. (luk– waka fɔ natin........)**
Literal Translation	The bottom does not give, it is the foot which gives.
Interpretation	You stand a better chance of gaining something if you are moving around, than if you are sitting down. Make an effort instead of just sitting idly expecting something to fall into your lap.
Exercise: Reader's Interpretation	
375. Krio Parebul	**wes se in masta fat yes se nɔ. (.....yes se na lay)**
Literal Translation	The bottom says its master farted, the ear says no.
Interpretation	One who is far away from the scene of action thinks he/she is better qualified to know what is happening than the person on the ground.
Exercise: Reader's Interpretation	
376. Krio Parebul	**wetin de pan nɛk ɛn wes we bid nɔ no. (luk– usay de pan yams.....)**
Literal Translation	What is on the neck and hips which beads do not know.

Interpretation	Someone proclaiming to know all about someone else's business, including all embarrassing titbits – has sexual innuendos.
Exercise: Reader's Interpretation	
377. Krio Parebul	**wetin dɔti man lɛk? pɔmp lɔk.**
Literal Translation	What does a dirty man like? Tap locked (ie. No running water)
Interpretation	One doesn't want to do something, and is happy when circumstances make it impossible or inconvenient for the exercise to be accomplished.
Exercise: Reader's Interpretation	
378. Krio Parebul	**wetin kɔba pɔsin, na pɔsin. wetin koba kola, na lif.**
Literal Translation	What covers a person, it is a person. What covers cola nut, it is a lif.
Interpretation	When in trouble, you need help from someone else. Nobody is self-sufficient.
Exercise: Reader's Interpretation	
379. Krio Parebul	**wetin ren mit na do, na in i go sok.**
Literal Translation	What rain meets outside is what it will soak.

Interpretation	You/it can only be affected if you are/it is in a vulnerable position.
Exercise: Reader's Interpretation	
380. Krio Parebul	**wɛn banana wan day, nain i de bɔn**
Literal Translation	When the banana tree is about to die, that is when it bears. (fruit)
Interpretation	A last burst of energy/effort at the very end, to rejuvenate a project.
Exercise: Reader's Interpretation	
381. Krio Parebul	**wɛn bɔlɔgi gɛt fat grɔn i kin prɛd.**
Literal Translation	When bology is in fertile soil, it spreads.
Interpretation	When conditions are very favourable, it is natural to seize the opportunity to flourish.
Exercise: Reader's Interpretation	
382. Krio Parebul	**wɛn ɛlifant fɛt, na di gras de sɔfa.**
Literal Translation	When the elephant fights, it is the grass that suffers.
Interpretation	When powerful people fight, ordinary people who are not involved in the quarrel, usually bear the brunt of the fight.
Exercise: Reader's Interpretation	

383. Krio Parebul	wɛn fish wan rɔtin, na frɔm di ed.
Literal Translation	When fish is about to rot, it starts from the head.
Interpretation	Corruption in society usually starts with the leadership.
Exercise: Reader's Interpretation	

384. Krio Parebul	wɛn snek dɔn bɛt yu, yu si rɔrɔm, yu go rɔn.
Literal Translation	When you have been bitten by a snake, you see a worm, you will run.
Interpretation	After an unpleasant experience, you are careful to avoid something similar. Once bitten, twice shy.
Exercise: Reader's Interpretation	

385. Krio Parebul	wɛn wata dɔn dɔti, i dɔn dɔti.
Literal Translation	When water is dirty, it is dirty.
Interpretation	The situation has passed the point of being remedied.
Exercise: Reader's Interpretation	

386. Krio Parebul	wi si tide wi nɔ si tumara.
Literal Translation	We see today, we do not see tomorrow.

Interpretation	Implied hope that the future will be better for the sufferer, and warning that the perpetraitor's actions might have dire repercussions.
Exercise: Reader's Interpretation	
387. Krio Parebul	**wɔd na fɔl eg.**
Literal Translation	Word is a fowl's egg.
Interpretation	Warning to think before you speak, because words which have been spoken cannot be 'unspoken'. – a broken egg can never be put back together.
Exercise: Reader's Interpretation	
388. Krio Parebul	**wɔd na mɔt nɔto lod na ed.**
Literal Translation	Word in the mouth is not a load on the head.
Interpretation	It is easy to talk. It is harder to do something.
Exercise: Reader's Interpretation	
389. Krio Parebul	**yay nɔ de si rawnd kɔna.**
Literal Translation	Eyes do not see round corners.
Interpretation	The position I'm in, there is no way I can know what's happening. I'm in no position to know the facts of this case.

Exercise: Reader's Interpretation	
390. Krio Parebul	**yay nɔ de tot lod, bɔt i no we i ebi. (yay nɔ gɛ skel bɔt i nɔ di lɔd we ebi.)**
Literal Translation	The eye does not carry a load, bɔt it knows when it is heavy.
Interpretation	Work can be accurately assessed without actual involvement.
Exercise: Reader's Interpretation	
391. Krio Parebul	**yes yɛri, mɔt sɛt.**
Literal Translation	Ear hears, mouth shuts.
Interpretation	Don't repeat everything you hear. Exercise control in keeping secrets.
Exercise: Reader's Interpretation	
392. Krio Parebul	**yu ayd yu bɔbi, ɔl yu wes de na do.(yu de fɛt fɔ ayd yu bɔbi....)**
Literal Translation	You are hiding your breasts, all of your bottom is outside. (exposed)
Interpretation	In your effort to hide one secret, you are unable to contain (conceal) much more damaging evidence.
Exercise: Reader's Interpretation	
393. Krio Parebul	**yu de ple jege wit dɛbul.**
Literal Translation	You are playing jege with a devil.

133

Interpretation	Negotiating with a formidable adversary, in his own field.
Exercise: Reader's Interpretation	
394. Krio Parebul	**yu de prɛd mata yu nɔ si man. (Luk– nɔ mek kata we lod nɔ de.)**
Literal Translation	You are spreading a mat, you haven't seen a man.
Interpretation	You are preparing for something which might never happen. Don't count your chickens before they are hatched.
Exercise: Reader's Interpretation	
395. Krio Parebul	**yu finga de na mi mɔt yu wan kɔnk mi ed.**
Literal Translation	Your finger is in my mouth you want to knock my head.
Interpretation	I am helping you and are in a position to hurt or even ruin you and you want to harm me?
Exercise: Reader's Interpretation	
396. Krio Parebul	**yu gi di kaw yu ol di rop.**
Literal Translation	You give the cow you hold the rope.

Interpretation	You ostensibly hand over, but are still calling the shots. You are being the power behind the throne.
Exercise: Reader's Interpretation	
397. Krio Parebul	**yu si sok lɛpɛt yu kɔl am pus.**
Literal Translation	You see a soaked leopard you call it puss.
Interpretation	You think someone very dangerous, is harmless.
Exercise: Reader's Interpretation	
398. Krio Parebul	**yu wan wan pit pan ol wɔl; if di ol wɔl pit pan yu, yu go sok. (if ol wɔl pit pan yu, yu go drawn).**
Literal Translation	You, on your own, want to spit at the whole world. If the whole world spits at you, you will get really wet.
Interpretation	You cannot antagonize everyone around you, because if they join forces and turn against you, you are bound to come out worse.
Exercise: Reader's Interpretation	

399. Krio Parebul	yu we put banga na faya, na yu go tek an pul am.
Literal Translation	You who put palm kernel inside fire, it is you who will take your hand to pull it out.
Interpretation	You have caused this dangerous situation, so you have to take the risk involved in sorting it out.
Exercise: Reader's Interpretation	
400. Krio Parebul	yuba nɔ gɛt pepa, bɔt i no wɛn fɔtide.
Literal Translation	The vulture does not have paper, but it knows when it is the traditional fortieth day ceremony.
Interpretation	Even though you did not tell me your business, I knew about it. There are many ways of getting information .
Exercise: Reader's Interpretation	

SIERRA LEONEAN WRITERS SERIES (SLWS)

Focusing on academic, fictional, and scientific writing that will complement other relevant materials used in schools, colleges, universities and other tertiary institutions, the Sierra Leonean Writers Series (SLWS) aims to promote good quality books by Sierra Leoneans writing on any topics and other writers from around the world who write on themes and issues about Sierra Leone.

It is the publisher's hope that students and other readers in Sierra Leone will eventually be at least some of the primary beneficiaries of these works. Not only will people in Sierra Leone be able to read materials that relate to their own lives and experiences, budding writers will also be able to draw inspiration from the efforts of their compatriots and other established writers.

Submitted work undergoes a rigorous peer-review process before being accepted for publication, with an international editorial board providing guidance to writers.

SLWS, based in Warima and Freetown in Sierra Leone, distributes books globally through AMAZON.COM. In Sierra Leone, SLWS books are currently available at the SLWS Bookshop in Warima (near Masiaka) and at CLC Bookshop, 92 Pademba Road in Freetown.

SLWS co-publishes some titles with Karantha Publishers in Sierra Leone.

For further information, please visit our website:
www.sl-writers-series.org
or contact the publisher, Prof. Osman A. Sankoh (Mallam O.)
publisher@sl-writers-series.org

Published Books – a milestone of the 50ᵗʰ title has been reached in September 2016!

1	Osman A. Sankoh (Mallam O.)	2001/ 2016	*A Memoir*	*Hybrid Eyes – An African in Europe*
2	Osman A. Sankoh (Mallam O.)	2001	*Non-fiction*	*Beautiful Colours*
3	Sheikh Umarr Kamarah	2002/ 2015	*Poems*	*Singing in Exile and The Child of War*
4	Abdul B. Kamara	2003/ 2015	*A Memoir*	*Unknown Destination*
5	Samuel Hinton	2003	*Poems*	*The Road to Kenema*
6	Karamoh Kabba	2005/ 2016	*A Novel*	*Morquee – The Political Drama of Wish over Wisdom*
7	Yema Lucilda Hunter	2007	*A Novel*	*Redemption Song*
8	Joe A. D. Alie	2007/ 2015	*Research Text*	*Sierra Leone Since Independence – History of a Postcolonial State*
9	Mohamed Combo Kamanda	2007	*A Play*	*The Visa*
10	J Sorie Conteh	2007	*A Novel*	*In Search of Sons*
11	Michael Fayia Kallon	2010/ 2015	*A Novel*	*The Ghosts of Ngaingah*
12	J Sorie Conteh	2011	*A Novel*	*Family Affairs*
13	Winston Forde	2011	*A Play*	*Layila, Kakatua wan bi Lida*
14	Eustace Palmer Doc P.	2012	*A Novel*	*A Pillar of the Community*
15	Siaka Kroma	2012	*Non-fiction*	*Manners Maketh Man – Adventures of a Bo School Boy*
16	Mohamed Combo Kamanda (ed)	2012	*Short Stories*	*The Price and other Short Stories from Sierra Leone*

17	Sigismond Tucker	2013	*A Memoir*	*From the Land of Diamonds to the Isle of Spice*
18	Bailah Leigh	2013	*Non-fiction*	*Dilemma of Freedom – A Diary from Behind Rebels Lines in the Sierra Leone Civil War*
19	Nnamdi Carew	2013	*A Novella*	*Tiger Fist – Two Stories*
20	Yema Lucilda Hunter	2013	*A Novel*	*Joy Came in the Morning*
21	Ebenezer 'Solo' Collier	2013	*Research Text*	*Primary & Secondary Education in Sierra Leone – Evaluation of more than 50 years of PRACTICES & POLICIES*
22	Gbananom Hallowell	2013	*Short Stories*	*Gbomgbosoro - Two Stories*
23	Sheikh Umarr Kamarah & Majorie Jones (eds)	2013	*Poems*	*beg sol noba kuk sup - An Anthology of Krio Poetry*
24	Siaka Kroma	2014	*Short Stories*	*Tales from the Fireside*
25	Syl Cheney-Coker*	2014	*Poems*	*The Road to Jamaica*
26	Dr Sama Banya	2015	*A Memoir*	*Looking Back – My Life and Times*
27	Andrew K Keili	2015	*Social Commentary*	*Ponder My Thoughts – Vol. 1*
28	Jedidah A. O. Johnson	2015	*A Novel*	*Youthful Yearnings*
29	Oumar Farouk Sesay	2015	*A Novel*	*Landscape of Memories*
30	Oumar Farouk Sesay	2015	*Poems*	*The Edge of a Cry*
31	Gbanabom Hallowell	2015	*A Novel*	*The Road to Kaibara*
32	Mohamed Gibril Sesay*	2015	*A Novel*	*This Side of Nothingness*
33	Yema Lucilda Hunter	2015	*A Novel*	*Nanna*

34	Yusuf Bangura	2015	*Research Text*	*Development, Democracy & Cohesion*
35	Lansana Gberie	2015	*Research Text*	*War, Politics & Justice in West Africa*
36	Yema Lucilda Hunter	2015	*A Biography*	*An African Treasure: In Search of Gladys Casely-Hayford 1904-1950*
37	Moses Kainwo	2015	*Poems*	*Ayo Ayo Ayo and other Love Songs*
38	Abdulai Walon-Jalloh	2015	*Poems*	*Voices and Passions*
39	Gbanabom Hallowell (Ed.)	2016	*Short Stories*	*In the Belly of the Lion – An Anthology of new Sierra Leonean Short Stories*
40	Ahmed Koroma	2016	*Poems*	*Along the Odokoko River - Poems*
41	George Coleridge-Taylor	2016	*A Memoir*	*Transformation in Transition*
42	Karamoh Kabba	2016	*Research Text*	*Fire from Timbuktu: A Dialogue with History*
43	Umu Kultumie Tejan-Jalloh	2016	*A Memoir*	*Telling It As It Was: The Career of A Sierra Leonean Woman in Public Service*
44	Ambrose Massaquoi	2016	*Poems*	*Along the Peal of Drums: Collected Poems (1990-2015)*
45	Mohamed Gibril Sesay	2016	*Poems*	*At the Gathering of Roads (Poems)*
46	Gbanabom Hallowell	2016	*Poems*	*Manscape in the Sierra: New and Collected Poems 1991-2011*
47	Gbanabom Hallowell (Ed.)	2016	*Short Stories and Poems*	*Leoneanthology: Comtemporary Short Stories and Poems from Sierra Leone*
48	Gbanabom Hallowell	2016	*Poems*	*Don't Call Me Elvis and Other Poems*
49	Bakar Mansaray	2016	*Short Stories*	*A Suitcase Full of Dried Fish and Other Stories*

| 50 | Gbanabom Hallowell | 2016 | *Poems* | *The Art of the Lonely Wanderer* |

*co-published with Karantha Publishers